IS-Abel

An Inspiring Story of Survival and Hope
Through Northern Ireland's Care System

Isabel Kelly

IS-Abel

An Inspiring Story of Survival and Hope
Through Northern Ireland's Care System

© Isabel Kelly, 2024

ISBN: 978-1-0686490-4-2

We print our book on forestry sustainable paper. Viva la forests!

Disclaimer

The content of this memoir is based on the author's recollections and experiences. Some names, locations, events, and dates have been altered or omitted to protect the privacy of individuals and to respect their confidentiality. The views and opinions expressed in this book are solely those of the author and do not reflect the views of the publisher.

This book is published with the understanding that the publisher is not engaged in rendering professional services. The publisher and the author are providing this memoir as is without any warranties or guarantees of any kind, either expressed or implied, regarding the completeness, accuracy, or reliability of the information contained within.

The publisher disclaims any liability in connection with the use of this information. Any reliance on the material in this book is at the reader's own risk. The publisher and the author shall not be held liable for any damages or losses arising from the use or misuse of the information provided in this memoir.

Any similarity to real persons, living or dead, is purely coincidental and not intended by the author. The book is intended for informational purposes only and does not constitute legal, medical, or other professional advice.

For professional advice, please consult a qualified professional.

Foreword by Isabel Kelly

It is with a sense of honour that I introduce my remarkable story, which sheds light on the unseen and unheard experiences of a child being brought up in the care system in Northern Ireland. Life brings us all on different journeys. What motivates us? What challenges us? What inspires us? In the tapestry of life, some threads are woven with more trials and tribulations than others. Growing up in the care system in Northern Ireland is an experience that few can fully comprehend and is a journey unlike any other. My journey is just one of many, but it is a voice among many that calls for compassion, understanding and respect.

In the heart of every child lies a story waiting to be told. My profound journey was marked by challenges and pain, highs and lows and moments of despair that tested me to the limit. I share my story not to just recount the challenges I faced, but to highlight the resilience, courage and hope that carried me through.

As you read through the pages, you will witness my raw and unfiltered experiences and struggles for identity and belonging, facing adversity head-on. Yet, amidst the challenges, you will see the transformation of my life once filled with uncertainty into one of purpose and fulfilment. Despite the odds I emerged stronger, more resilient, and determined to carve out a life filled with hope and possibility.

My journey is not just about survival; it was about thriving, finding strength in vulnerability, and to find my own voice – a voice that had been silenced for too long. I have used my voice for those who feel unheard and a beacon of hope for those who feel lost. Every child, no matter how broken or lost, has the potential for transformation.

This foreword is not just an introduction to my story; it is a celebration of my ability to overcome adversity, adapt and thrive. Our past does not define us; it is our response to it that shapes our future.

Dedication

I want to dedicate this book to survivors and victims of Historical Abuse and children who are in or who have left the foster care system. There is HOPE.

I want to thank Niall from ShadowScript Ghostwriters, who mentored and supported me on the journey of this book. From our initial contact, his unwavering commitment, passion, and enthusiasm for me to publish this book made it so much easier than I ever imagined. When I received his first email stating – *"My work schedule may not match yours—please do not feel obliged to reply outside of your normal working hours."* I laughed out loud and hard, thinking I am not a '9-5' type of girl and I hope he doesn't mind receiving emails late into the night! His precision and professionalism in editing, ghostwriting, and designing my book have been nothing but outstanding. He has always wanted the best for me and more, providing me with advice and information that went outside of his remit. Niall, sincerely, I cannot thank you enough and sincerely appreciate everything you have done for me. I never made that trip west! I want to thank Conor from ShadowScript Ghostwriters, who joined us both in the latter stage of the publishing and marketing of my book. Your input and attention to detail has been exemplary. I look forward to working with you after I launch my book.

Thank you to my dear friend who helped me put my book together all those years ago and laid the foundations for my book. You were the very person to bring it to my attention that my name was actually IS-Abel. You were a genius and I give you all the praise for the naming of my book.

Thank you to all the family and friends, who I interviewed for my book. Your honesty and input have been invaluable, and I love you all dearly.

Thank you to all my family and friends who have listened to me bend their ears for years about me wanting to write a book. I am sure you are glad I have finally done it. Your patience has been appreciated. Can you believe I got there in the end?

Thank you to Rosie, my dedicated health and wellbeing caseworker at Wave Trauma Centre, for all the support, help and kindness you have shown me and for signposting me to ShadowScript Ghostwriters. Thank you to Victims and Survivors Service. I really appreciate everything you have done for me.

A massive thank you to my son-in-law, Noah, who has helped and continued to help me with my marketing. I'm sure when you gained a mother-in-law you never thought I would rope you in for favours so quickly!

I want to thank our incredible four beautiful children Tierna, Ross, Craig and Calvin for just being you. A special thank you goes to Calvin who allowed me to share his story. You are so brave. Children, you have all brought me so much joy and happiness to my life and I am incredibly proud of each and one of you. I know I don't tell you enough, but I love you beyond anything.

And finally, but not least, my wonderful husband Roy. Thank you for supporting me in this journey, listening to me harp on about my book for *years*, discussing the draft and bending your ear late into the morning. Nothing is ever too much for you. You are truly a remarkable husband who always has my interests at heart. My love for you goes beyond words.

About This Book

Embark on an extraordinary journey of resilience, triumph, and profound self-discovery with Isabel Kelly, a woman who defied the odds stacked against her in the heart-wrenching memoir, *IS-Abel - An Inspiring Story of Survival and Hope Through Northern Ireland's Care System.* Isabel's life began in the harsh embrace of the Northern Ireland care system, abandoned by her mother at just four months old. As she reached the pivotal age of 50, a question from her husband on a sunlit spring morning sparked a profound reflection: What could, or would, she do differently with her life?

In this riveting narrative, Isabel unveils a tapestry woven with threads of trauma, emotional and physical abuse, separation, rejection, insecurity, and grief. Yet, amidst the shadows of her past, Isabel illuminates the pages with a beacon of hope. With a candid and courageous spirit, she shares her longing for comprehensive support from professionals to navigate the labyrinth of her emotions, something that extended for three tumultuous decades.

Wishing she had forgiven her abusers and detractors sooner in life, Isabel's journey becomes a testament to the transformative power of forgiveness. The burden of bitterness, anger, and resentment, carried for far too long, threatened to eclipse her potential. Despite failing her O' Levels and GCSE's twice, Isabel's unwavering determination prevailed. Against all odds, she emerged as the ***first foster child*** in the Down and Lisburn Trust now known as South Eastern Health and Social Care Trust to graduate at university level, proving that resilience knows no bounds.

This book is not merely a tale of survival; it is a celebration of the human spirit's indomitable will to thrive. Isabel's story will inspire, captivate, and resonate with readers, leaving an indelible mark long after the last page is turned. Join Isabel on a remarkable journey from despair to triumph, and discover the extraordinary strength that lives within us all.

Table of Contents

Section 1

The Early Years

Getting it Right

IN THE REALM OF care services, maintaining accurate personal details is crucial for establishing a foundation of trust between providers and clients, and is something we might well take for granted. Why? Well, this trust is essential for fostering positive outcomes. As you can imagine, getting things right in someone's personal details plays a huge role in many aspects of client care, including administration, treatment and intervention plans, and indeed, overall quality of care. When data is precise and reliable, care staff and all other professionals in the life of a child, and teen can deliver a more human and holistic approach. It's not too much to ask that meticulous documentation and verification of personal information are a matter of daily practice to promote effective administration and overall quality of care in social care settings.

Did this happen for me? No, it did not. Unbelievably, something as basic as getting my name right was too much for those entrusted with my care and this has had a lifelong effect on me.

My name is ISABEL. And this is my story.

Trauma

FROM THE AGE OF 4 months, I experienced early-life adversity, being separated from both my biological parents and brother and sister. The distress of the separation in itself and not bonding with any of my parents and siblings at a crucial stage of my development, resulted in me experiencing a series of traumatic emotional reactions throughout my childhood, teen years and into adulthood. From the moment I started to talk and become familiar with my surroundings, I was acutely aware that my living environment at the baby home where I lived was certainly not normal.

Children who enter the care of state services, whether due to abuse, neglect, or an inability of their birth families to care for them, often endure experiences that can have long-term emotional and psychological consequences. Being placed in foster care, residential care, or other forms of state custody frequently leads to feelings of abandonment. For many of these children, this early sense of rejection and instability manifests into deeper mental health challenges in adulthood, including profound anxiety and emotional detachment. Abandonment is one of the most prevalent emotional experiences faced by children in state care. The very act of being separated from their birth family, even when necessary for their safety, can trigger feelings of rejection, confusion, and loss. Children develop a sense of security from stable, nurturing relationships. When that security is disrupted, either by the removal from their family or frequent moves between different foster homes, the child's sense of self-worth is often damaged.

Children who experience abandonment often carry these feelings into adulthood. One of the most common manifestations of this early trauma is chronic anxiety. A study published by Perry and Szalavitz (2021) found that adults who experienced unstable care environments during childhood were more likely to develop anxiety disorders later in life. The

4

unpredictability of their early environment often leads to hypervigilance, a heightened sense of alertness to potential threats, even in situations where no immediate danger exists. This heightened anxiety can permeate various aspects of life, from professional settings to personal relationships.

Equally concerning is the emotional detachment that often develops in individuals who grew up in state care. When children endure repeated emotional disruptions—moving from one home to another, or never forming a strong, supportive bond with a caregiver—they can become emotionally numb as a form of self-protection. A study by Goldman, Salus, Wolcott, and Kennedy (2022) showed that these individuals often struggle to form and maintain intimate relationships in adulthood, fearing emotional closeness due to past experiences of rejection or instability. The emotional walls they build during childhood as a means of coping with their trauma persist into adulthood, making it difficult for them to trust others or fully engage in relationships.

While the long-term effects of being in state care can be severe, it is crucial to recognise that early intervention can help mitigate these outcomes. Trauma-informed care and therapeutic support, provided consistently throughout a child's time in the system, can reduce feelings of abandonment and help children develop healthier coping mechanisms.

Research by Dozier and Rutter (2021) emphasises the importance of stable, supportive environments for children in care, as well as ongoing mental health support. They argue that providing children with consistent, nurturing relationships can reduce the likelihood of anxiety and emotional detachment in adulthood. Foster care systems that prioritise these needs, focusing not only on the child's immediate safety but also on their long-term emotional well-being, can help break the cycle of trauma. But, not always as we will come to learn in my book.

My time preceding the baby home, the children's home, was definitely not normal. There, I experienced physical and emotional abuse, and was sexually abused by a stranger on the grounds of the tennis courts. Unbelievably, no one ever came to my aid to comfort me, reassure me, or even tell me they loved me during this time. I tried my best to be a 'good' girl and even though I was good most of the time, I was punished by Sister Angus. Living in such a harsh and cruel environment I was always hyper-vigilant, vulnerable, fearful and worried. I found it incredibly difficult to process my emotions and, would react by lashing out, only to find myself in a far worse situation. I trusted no one, nor did I confide in a soul, it was a sad and pathetic existence.

Despite the trauma I endured at the children's home, when I reached adulthood, I *returned* many times over the years to visit the Mother Superior. I was inexplicably drawn back to visit this woman, this surrogate mother, an attachment that I had formed that could not easily be shaken off. I knew nothing different as it was a place that had been my 'home' for the first seven years of my life.

The Mother Superior welcomed me with open arms and was always delighted to see me. She took great interest in what I was doing and reminisced about the 'good aul days', well that's what she seemed to perceive of our shared experiences. My last visit there was in 2019; she was now her in her nineties and living in an older person's accommodation. She asked me if I wanted to visit Nazareth Lodge, now replaced with an older person's home run by the Sisters of Nazareth. Before I knew it, we were travelling back to the place I was so desperate to leave all those years ago.

Entering the gates, I was suddenly hit with an array of memories and flashbacks, desperately trying to visualise buildings and gardens that once occupied the land. The Mother Superior in her frail state moved briskly in her rollator to bring me to the beautiful chapel, now an older people's care home, where she pointed out different statues that once stood previously in Nazareth Lodge. I couldn't help but notice the sadness in her face and the realisation how things had incredibly changed for her life since the closure of the children's home. I was taken aback by how sharp her mind was, telling me how well-mannered and well-behaved I was as a child. She told me her days were busy leaving me to Nursery School, then hopping on a bus to work at another Nursery School, then hurrying back to collect me. Eventually, she moved to the same Nursery School I went to. When I left the children's home, I never dared to mention my experiences because I felt no one would believe me and I was too afraid of people's reactions.

As I reached the puberty stage, I found it incredibly difficult to process what happened to me and was easily triggered by what people said, did or, indeed, by different situations I would find myself in. This caused me to be irrational often reacting inappropriately because of my frustrations, sadness, anger, and irritability. I struggled massively with insecurity, rejection and jealousy, always being defensive and seeking people's approval, which culminated in lingering feelings of low self-worth, loneliness and deep sadness. I was never encouraged to talk about my feelings, nor did anyone ever identify that I was struggling. Sometimes my body would be so dysregulated with my heart beating so fast purely because I did not have the proper emotional regulation skills and strategies to manage my behaviour. My schoolwork suffered where I lost interest in my education, dropping exams because I could not be bothered anymore. At that time, I did not know it was trauma I was experiencing.

In response to my erratic behaviour, I turned to smoking and drinking alcohol in my late teens to numb my pain and calm my nervous system. I was desperate to belong to someone or something and to be loved.

When I was in my late teens, I took an interest in the younger, fostered children in the family and children from the extended family I was part of. I put their needs first and did a range of activities with them such as adventure walks, camping and going to the cinema. They became my pride and joy, encouraging and inspiring them to see their worth and how brilliant they were. To this day, I still have a strong relationship with some of the children, now grown into beautiful adults. I feel my time and encouragement was well worth it and instrumental in the development of their lives, even for only a small part. So many of the children had difficulties like myself, but have gone and made a success and a great life for themselves.

7

Just before my fortieth birthday, I went searching for my biological mother. I knew she had lived on and off at Purdysburn Hospital in Belfast most of her life because of her poor mental health, so I tried there first. I explained my situation to an employee and was put through gruelling questions to identify who I was.

My mother was found. Two days later, with bags of presents, I nervously drove to a nursing home in Belfast along with my Aunt Kathleen to meet my mother. I was excited but anxious about meeting her. Greeted by the matron in charge at the nursing home where my mother was now living, I showed her a photograph of *my* mother.

To my horror, the woman I was about to meet was not my mother. She was someone else's mother. But not mine. How could the hospital get it so wrong? Where was *my* mother? I was desperate to find answers.

So, let's go back to the very beginning-1971.

Handed Over to the State

BEING IN THE CARE OF state services, while often a necessary intervention, can leave children feeling abandoned, a wound that frequently manifests as profound anxiety and emotional detachment in adulthood. By better recognising the emotional toll that state care can take, and addressing it with targeted strategies, we can help children in care not only survive their circumstances but thrive as adults. I am fortunate that I am in the latter category, but it could have been so different if I was not such a resilient character.

Born on the 30th of March 1971, in Malone Place Maternity Hospital in Belfast, I was given the name Isobel Flynn. My father was barely in his twenties when he was left alone with the daunting responsibility of raising five children, me being the youngest, after my mother had deserted us. The struggle became overwhelming, and after enduring three days of single parenthood, a momentous decision was made. On that fateful 3rd of August in 1971, my siblings and I were unceremoniously surrendered to the State's embrace.

The twist in this familial tale goes deeper than just a father's inability to confide in his own kin. Unbeknownst to anyone, our existence remained shrouded in secrecy, concealed from his family. It wasn't until desperation gripped him, compelling him to seek aid, that the truth about us emerged.

Imagine the astonishment that rippled through his family, especially my Aunt Kathleen, a confidante who believed she knew him inside out. In that moment of revelation, she found herself caught in a web of familial complexities. Juggling her own domestic responsibilities, she couldn't rescue us from our dire straits. In a heart-wrenching revelation years later, Aunt Kathleen disclosed the grim reality of our condition when we were discovered. We were not just abandoned; we were dirty, unkempt, and hunger-stricken. The news shattered her compassionate heart, leaving an indelible mark on the narrative of our shared past. This has stayed with me my entire life.

So, there I was placed in the hands of nuns who looked after destitute children. I had no say in this matter as my father was a Roman Catholic and obviously made the decision that I would be one, too. To make it easier for the nuns and convenient to manage their workload, they had already made their decision that they were going to separate siblings at St Joseph's baby home. Why would my situation be any different? Despite being separated from my mother and father, these cruel nuns did not care if I was separated from siblings at a crucial stage of my life. But that wasn't even the worst of it. Somehow, someone, *anyone,* neglected to tell me I even had a brother and sister, or that they were being raised in the same building that I was occupying.

Life continued until one day, aged 17 months, I was randomly selected unbeknown to me, by a worker who was instructed by the nuns to bring a destitute child home for the weekend. This was to be my first place of normality where I was welcomed by a family with open arms and who would love me unconditionally. I even called the workers parents 'mum' and 'dad'. I too, inherited the name 'Wee Bizz', which just summed my entire personality up to a tee, chatty, busy, energetic and inquisitive.

The estrangement from my brother and sister continued until the worker who took me home at the weekends had arranged a second birthday party for me in the baby home. Out of the blue, another asked her if my brother and were sister invited? In complete astonishment, she had not realised that I had siblings and insisted that they too were to be invited. On a joyous occasion, all three of us were united for the first time. After this exciting news, the worker told her father that I had a brother and sister, and he insisted that they too join me on weekends at their home. And that was the beginning of three of us being together escaping the realms of institute living and staying with a proper family at the weekends.

Four months after my 3rd birthday, the nun's broke protocol and placed my sister and me together with my brother who had already moved into Nazareth Lodge, a children's home next to the baby home. That was the first time we were all together, strangers simply battling to survive. We were looked after by the Mother Superior, a woman in her late forties, stout, wore glasses and, typical of the times, wearing the older Irish woman's uniform of a blouse and skirt. She had joined Nazareth Lodge in 1958.

The Mother Superior worked from 6 am to 10 pm every day, sometimes until 11 pm if she had to lock up after a meeting. Plus, of course, she worked above the shop as the saying goes, living in the Lodge. She never married and had all the time in the world to work over and above her hours. The Mother Superior was strict in looking after her whippets, running everything to clockwork and ruling with a firm hand. A caretaker brought up in Nazareth Lodge called us 'Seven little whippets, big and strong, the Mother Superior (her name) owns them all'. I had not the faintest idea what a whippet was back then, so I just laughed at the thrill of someone owning me, at my young age. The Mother Superior was a perfectionist, demanded high standards and was controlling. I was naïve to think she was a bad person, evil or vindictive and saw no harm when she slapped me which was incredibly painful or chastised me for misbehaving. This was common practice at the time in wider society and I genuinely believe she did not see any harm in this. I did not know any different and had become acquainted with the rules and regimes of institutional living. Who was I to question? Despite all her failings, she was the FIRST mother figure in my young life that I so desperately craved for who taught me manners. The idea of ever letting me outside to play at such a young age was never an option, simply because there was no one to look after me and I was too young to go alone. So, I spent my time and a lot of that on the living room herringbone floor on my own, playing with donated toys and dolls. Playing with dolls was my favourite, pretending I was the mum looking after my children. How I yearned even then to have a mummy who I was yet to meet. The loss was enormous. Sometimes, we were allowed to watch television. My favourite programme was Little House on the Prairie. So just to be like

Laura Ingalls I got the Mother Superior to plait my long brown hair. I was infatuated with her and wanted what she had: a mum, dad and siblings who were kept together, she was seemingly very happy. At the very end of the programme, Laura, with her two long plaits and beautiful freckly face runs through the beautiful meadows and at the very end raises her two arms and more or less takes off like a bird. How I yearned to be like her, not a care in the world and free as a bird. In some episodes, I cried uncontrollably. Not because it was sad but because of the insurmountable loss of not being part of a family.

Bath time was something else, clambering up over the kitchen units to get into the Belfast sink for the Mother Superior to wash my hair and body with carbolic soap that stank and stung like hell when it went into my eyes. She was too busy rushing to hear or see the laugher and nosiness of children peeking through the window at me. This woman did not care about my dignity or feelings of embarrassment as she was too busy and engrossed in her own work.

Bed time was early, with no consideration given to brighter evenings. I shared a large dormitory with another 6 children; boys and girls. Conveniently, I slept on the second bed to the left with my siblings sleeping either side. In the middle of the night, my sleep was always disturbed when the Mother Superior would switch the bright light on that hurt my eyes to wake us all up to go to the toilet. That was to avoid us from wetting the bed, which I occasionally did. To my dismay she would wake us all up at the same time and instruct us to queue in an orderly line outside the bathroom, one by one taking turns then returning to bed struggling to fall back to sleep.

I started Bethlehem Nursery School aged 3, which coincidently was on the same grounds of the children's home. The Poor Sisters of Nazareth set up the Nursery School and St Michael's Primary School in 1974, so destitute children from the home could go. It had to be open to the public to get funding. I have no recollection of being told I was starting Nursery School or being brought to get a new uniform, shoes and school bag like parents would do with their children. On my first day, I was greeted by a peculiar nun who was dressed in a white habit with

12

a fancy whinged thing over her head. Her whole demeanour threw me, as she was nice and pleasant to me, not like the nuns I came across in the home. I loved everything about Nursery School though bouts of sadness would raise its head, mainly because I did not have a mummy and daddy to bring me to and collect me from nursery and be fixated with their pride and joy. I felt alone, and yes there were other children there, probably about 30 of them, and the nuns, of course. But they weren't my family, my real family. It was me all alone, trying to muddle through my thoughts of the emptiness of not belonging to a family. Little did I know I would carry this feeling throughout my childhood and into my adulthood.

In September 1975, I was old enough to start St Michael's Primary School. I was really excited to be starting school but was also nervous about meeting new friends and worried if anyone would find out that I lived in a children's home. I had real big hang ups by then and struggled to find the reason my mother had never come to visit me. Was I that bad? I was told years later that my mother had visited occasionally with my grandmother. Likewise, my father, grandparents, and two aunts visited. I have no memories of them ever visiting me. All I ever thought at that age was nobody cared about me. Going to school was the highlight of my day. I walked down the lane with other children from the home, hung my coat up in the cloakroom and went to my classroom. No kisses, hugs or goodbyes. At school, I could be myself and play and interact with other 'normal' children. At such a young age, I had a hunger to learn and now as an adult that remains with me. I doubt the other children knew anything about me. It was never ever spoken about. I was too engrossed in learning, playing and having a good time. Often, I returned home from school alone, engrossed in my thoughts about being reunited with my mum and dad. Once I reached the door to the lodge, my thoughts would vanish and I was back to institutional living, rules and regimes.

At 5, I was told I was moving groups. My haven with the Mother Superior for the last 2 years was ending. Despite all Mother Superior's wrongdoings, I was saddened to leave. I had formed an attachment with her and was afraid that the bond would be broken. I begged her to come and see me and keep in touch. I seldom saw her after that. I was absolutely devastated when I moved into Sister Angus' group. My new group was on the second floor above the chapel. Moving from a group of seven children to a bigger group of 20 plus was a massive shock to my system. Then, on top of that, I was separated from my brother because of their stupid rules of putting girls into their sleeping quarters and boys into theirs.

Sister Angus was a horrible person. She was a big, hefty woman with a scowl on her face as if the world owed her. She entered the congregation in 1929 and died in 97. She worked at Nazareth Lodge from 1952 to 93, yes, 41 years. No wonder why she was miserable. In 1960 she became principal of the school and remained in that role until the two schools of Nazareth Lodge and Nazareth House were amalgamated and a new school was formed in 1974, St Michael's Primary School.

So, my new way of living was changing beyond my eyes. Aged 5 I was considered to be more responsible and therefore, was ordered that I would take on new chores, something I got away with at Mother Superior's group. And on top of that there were more rules but they were much worse. I was told that I wasn't allowed to watch television because it interfered with dinner time. My world had suddenly crashed and was about to end, because without Little House on the Prairie how was I ever going to function? To my despair, I cried wolf to the worker who was still taking me out at the weekends off-loading my burdens onto her. She was horrified to hear my awful news and intervened on my behalf. I was spared the trauma and in fact could watch it once a week in the comfort of Mother Superior's own living room. However, my one hour of heaven was over blitzed with more trauma that came my way.

To be fair, I was a well-behaved child, though very talkative. This got me into trouble loads of times where Sister Angus would hit me hard with her knuckles or hand and slapped me across the head, which throbbed for ages and made me dizzy. My sister and I often quarrelled over silly things but it did not help that I was very bossy and my sister always retaliated, which got us both into more trouble. It was always my way or nothing when we were playing and although my sister seldom gave in; we ended up quarrelling and disagreeing, which took up a good part of the time. Typical sisters at that age. Instead of the staff sorting our sibling rivalry they would get Sister Angus. She would appear from nowhere in her angry, high-pitched voice and hit and beat us with her bare hands. That was a regular occurrence, but none of the staff hit me. To my dismay, I always ended up the worst but never appeared to learn.

One afternoon, my sister and I were fighting. From nowhere, Sister Angus came roaring up the corridor to the both of us. She instructed us both to go into the kitchen along with another staff member. I was standing in trepidation in the corner while she dragged my sister by the ponytail across the room, calling her a crocodile. My poor sister was in an awful way, crying uncontrollably and yelling at her to stop. My body was in shock and my heart was beating forty to the dozen. All I could think was that I was going to be her next victim. Someone was looking over me that day as I miraculously escaped the beatings. I honestly feared for my life, as that woman scared the living daylights out of me.

Mealtimes were challenging, too. It was prepared by kitchen staff on the ground floor who would bring it up in a trolley whilst all the food in the containers was colour coded depending on what group you were in. At 5 years old, lost in my own thoughts, I would set the tables in the dining room while the older children served the food. The food was stinking and if not eaten; it was brought the next day and served to us in a miraculous dish called "bubble and squeak". All the leftovers put together, that you would not even serve to a dog. The only proper meal I would get was from free school dinners. My belly would rumble all the time simply because I was underfed and undernourished. But who was to care?

Instead of my dinner, I often ate sugar sandwiches and put 5 sugars in my tea. Sweets were a rarity and this was to be my sugar hit. Aged 5, I had to take my turn in washing the dishes in the neighbouring kitchen. Barely able to reach the sink, I stood on a chair washing all the dirty dishes while my clothes got drenched in the pursuit.

Little did I fathom the toothy consequences lurking in the sugary abyss of my childhood cravings. The sweet escapades of my early years, unbeknownst to me, would pave the way for a lifelong struggle with dental issues.

At 6, I found myself embarked on an ominous bus ride, a journey not of exploration but of dental reckoning. The destination? The dentist's chair, where 3 of my milky teeth were destined for extraction. This wasn't just a routine visit; it was a plunge for me into an abyss of fear, an ordeal that would haunt the corridors of my memory for years to come.

The anticipation hung heavy in the air, and as the dental chair loomed before me, a shiver of dread ran down my spine. To compound the anxiety, a stoic staff member escorted me, yet their presence offered no solace. Not a single word of comfort escaped their lips, leaving me to grapple with my mounting apprehension.

The dental proceedings unfolded like a silent horror film, each pull and tug resonating through my vulnerable senses. The aftermath was no less harrowing, as I stood there, blood-stained and defenceless, abandoned in the aftermath of my dental ordeal. That traumatic day has been etched into my memory, manifesting itself as an enduring fear that lingers. The mere mention of dentists triggers a chilling memory, a ghost from my past that refuses to be exorcised.

Into the realm of Sister Angus's dominion I ventured, an unwitting pawn in what I now perceive to be her sinister game. The Mother Superior, privy to my fear of the shadows, had passed this morsel of vulnerability to the very nun who would exploit it with a malevolence that echoed through the darkened corridors of my nights. Precisely when and how my nocturnal terror took root in my soul remains a mystery, but its relentless grip persists into my adult years. The very notion of surrendering to the abyss of darkness sends tremors through my being, compelling me to seek refuge. What a terrible legacy!

Sister Angus, however, harboured no sympathy for my phobia. Instead, she wielded it as a weapon, a tool to torment me with during the darkest hours. In the fiery storms of her wrath, if the whispers of my dormitory companions dared to rise above a hushed murmur or if our childlike antics dared disturb the sanctity of bedtime, she would ruthlessly slam shut the door that had been my lifeline, shutting out the comforting beams of light.

Nights transformed into a symphony of my silent sobs; a desperate lullaby sung to the tune of my fear. The oppressive darkness became a canvas for the cruel brushstrokes of Sister Angus's tyranny. In those moments of profound isolation, the cold reality set in on this vast earth, that there was no one to whom I could pour out the depths of my suffering. Alone, abandoned, and shrouded in the inky blackness, I sought solace where there was none, clinging to fragments of elusive comfort amid the malevolence of that unholy woman. The very essence of my fear became the instrument of my nightly agony, leaving scars in and on me that would linger long, long, after the lights had been extinguished.

While fast asleep one night, I was wakened by the sounding of a door closing. To my despair, I was getting punished again, but this time it was not my fault. I was left in complete darkness, oblivious to the world around me. I begged for the door to be opened again, but I was ordered back into bed. I had not a clue what was going on. With tears running down my eyes, I eventually fell asleep.

Suddenly, I was wakened by the command from Sister Angus' voice to get out of bed and come to the bathroom. My body felt disorientated. I'd no idea what I was called for in the middle of the night along with the rest of the girls in the dormitory. As I entered the bathroom, I could hear the cries of the other girls. What was going on? We were ordered individually to queue in a line and asked, were we talking? For every girl who lied, they got severely beaten with a slipper. It was then my turn. There was no way I was getting hit, so I told a lie and said that I was indeed talking. To my dismay, I was shoved harshly across the room and told, 'no you were not. You were sleeping.' Being brought up in this harsh environment it was always drummed into me that if I lied, then it was a sin and

God would punish me. I know you are probably thinking, so what, it is not a big deal? But it was to me back then. Even though the nuns were cruel to me, I idolised their teachings and, in my heart, I had sinned because I lied. What sort of way is that to bring up a child? Instead of not addressing it as a child I carried a lot of guilt for a long time with no one to confide with.

My brother, who was 2 and a half years older, had become a stranger to me. I never played with him and really only saw him at mealtimes. In the boys' quarters one night all of them were getting up to no good, probably bored as they were put to bed early. In the middle of the night, Sister Angus, in her fit of rage instructed him to polish all the shoes. Being horrified by her reaction he mischievously polished the shoes wrong. However funny he thought it was, she had other plans, and severely beat my brother like a rag doll. I was deeply shocked and saddened. She was an evil twisted animal.

Being raised by devout Catholic nuns who saw no failures in their wrongdoings, they ordered us every night to kneel and say our prayers and ask God for forgiveness in front of the Sacred Heart of Jesus statue. The demand to kneel upright for 30 minutes was cruel to any child. I struggled with this and would simply kneel on my honkers to give my poor legs a rest. To my horror, Sister Angus would slap me across my head with her bare hands for me to get up, which would then throb for a long time afterwards. I had so much hatred for this woman. As subsequent punishment, I was ordered to go to Mass the next morning in the chapel on the floor below.

Along with the harsh living conditions came a wee bit of enjoyment. I was allowed to play outside unsupervised. Playing outdoors was my escape from the realms of rules and abuse and sometimes, I would be by myself with not a care in the world. One sunny afternoon aged 6, I was outside playing on my own. Boredom set in, so I ventured into the tennis courts, which were out of bounds for us children from the home. I did not care about breaking the rules and was sure no one would ever find out. There was no one there so, I sat on a bench that overlooked the tennis courts. Dreaming of actually playing tennis and in a world of my own, a complete stranger, came and sat beside me. I knew there and then that I needed to get away. Within minutes, he presented a needle to me and asked me to hold it for him. I was speechless and shook my head. Thrust upon me, he put his hand up the inside of my leg and touched my private parts. My body was shaking uncontrollably and I was petrified. Inside my head, I was screaming. I knew this situation was unsafe. Then, literally within seconds, this stranger, a male, forced his body onto mine, trying to do things I cannot write about here, but I'm sure you can guess. Within seconds, he released his heavy body from mine and in that moment; I escaped from his reach, running for my life. Horrified about what had happened, my body was in utter shock.

But that was not the rest of it. I could tell no one my secret. I had broken the rules and even though my ordeal was horrific, getting punished was even worse. However, while running up the corridor in floods of tears I bumped into the Mother Superior who was shocked to see me crying. I did not want to confide in her. How could I? To get her trust I asked her if I told her, would she promise I would not get punished? She reassured me that I would not.

I was taken into the visitor's room and the police were called. Two lovely police officers interviewed me about the incident. After my tremendous ordeal, I was simply let go and told to go back to the group. On that horrific day, not one person consoled me, put their arms around me or reassured me that it would be okay. Everyone saw how traumatised I was. For a long time after, I found it incredibly difficult to regulate my emotions and had a fear of going outside. In the days and weeks after, not one person ever checked in with me. Not being able to talk about that incident or my emotions only give me one option. The only way I was ever going to toughen up and survive was to suppress my emotions. Now that I am older, I have learnt that by not dealing with my trauma it would eventually raise its head, with flashbacks and resentment towards the very people who failed me as a child.

So, life resumed to what I can call normal after that. My outbursts became more erratic simply because I could not manage my emotions, which subsequently lead me to getting physically and emotionally abused by Sister Angus So, my turmoil of abuse continued.

As a child, obsessed with chocolate and all things sweet, Christmas time was a joyous occasion. Some of the local taxi firms took pity on us 'destitute children' at the children's home. Picking us up in black taxis, they took us to Christmas parties in Belfast. It was like Charlie and the Chocolate Factory with all the sweets and chocolates. My eyes were bigger than my belly, eating loads of sweets and chocolates and being allowed to fill a bag for my return. While entering the lodge with my belly full, ribs sore from laughter and high from all the sugar I consumed, my joyous occasion would come to an abrupt end.

I would be told to be quiet by the nuns and my large bag of sweets and chocolate snatched from my reach never to be seen again. And this is a metaphor for my life; being so close to something or someone and yet so far. Why did it have to be so?

Summer Time Memories

THE SCORCHING SUMMERS OF 1974 to 1977 unfurled a tapestry of freedom for a young soul, as we were spirited away to an RAF billet camp at Ballyhornan for sun-soaked escapades. The barracks held our dreams as we slumbered in one and feasted in another, the promise of boundless adventure lingering in the air.

At a mere 6 years old, I found myself amidst the intoxicating heat, clad in shorts and a t-shirt, oblivious to the notion of the importance of using sun cream to protect our sensitive Celtic skins. The world opened up before me, a vast playground where the reins of supervision loosened, granting us the exhilarating liberty to explore the countryside unsupervised.

Memories of that summer still dance like sunbeams in my mind. The searing heat embraced me as I frolicked along the sandy shores, my shorts and t-shirt doubling as the unofficial uniform of freedom. The blissful hours slipped away, with no care for towels or convention, as I plunged into the water with reckless abandon.

The small shop and petrol pumps beckoned, becoming a makeshift haven for my youthful hunger. The locals, benevolent guardians of my transient joy, sometimes gifted me with sweets and ice cream, their kindness transcending any awareness I may have had of my origin in the children's home. In those moments, the world felt boundless, and their generosity became the sweet soundtrack to my summer symphony.

A quaint cottage nestled nearby, home to Mrs. Magee, became a treasure trove as I collected eggs in a wooden basket. The simplicity of that act resonated with joy, a stark departure from the rigid routine of institutional living.

As the days unfolded in a kaleidoscope of joy and liberation, the camp became a sanctuary from the confines of the children's home. I revelled in the freedom, the taste of a life unshackled. Reluctance clung to my heart as the days dwindled and the inevitable end loomed on the horizon. In the embrace of that summer I discovered a respite from institutional walls, a fleeting chapter that, in my heart, I wished would never close.

The only two good memories I have salvaged from the children's home were being allowed to watch the TV show, Little House on the Prairie and go out to the workers' home at the weekends. Even though I lived in the city of Belfast, I was in my cocoon at the lodge. Once we drove out of those gates most Friday nights to go to the country for the weekend, I felt a huge relief dreaming that I would never have to return. That dream did eventually become a reality. The worker who had taken me home during those weekends when I was a baby eventually fostered all three of us with her new husband. On the 14th of March 1978, a Parental Rights Order was enforced.

I officially belonged to the State, rejected by both my parents who no longer wanted anything more to do with me. End of.

Living in Foster Care

ON THE 14th of APRIL 1978, just after my 7th birthday, all three of us left Nazareth Lodge for good to live permanently with our new foster parents. That memory has been ingrained in me all my life. Before my big release into freedom, such a fuss was made over us. Photographs with the Mother Superior, Sister Angus, and the sister in charge were taken in the very garden we were never allowed to access all those years. Following protocol, we were required to go into the living room (Holy Room, I called it) to be officially released and provided with a reminder of a discharged receipt. The Mother Superior was in floods of tears. I was super hyper, and happy beyond anything I imagined. Finally, I was going to live with a proper family, a mum and dad who would take care of me, and love me unconditionally. Swooping up the drive one last time, I gazed into St Joseph's Baby Home, thinking I would never see it again. A massive relief suddenly enveloped me as I was escaping from this hellhole. The only home I knew in my first 7 years of my life.

Foster care plays a crucial role in providing stability, care, and protection to vulnerable children and young people who cannot live with their birth families. In Northern Ireland, the foster care system is an essential component of child welfare, offering a temporary safe haven while long-term solutions are sought. Circumstances may include neglect, abuse, family breakdown, or parental illness. Foster carers step in to provide a nurturing environment, aiming to meet the emotional, educational, and social needs of the child. There are both positive and negative aspects of foster care.

One of the most significant benefits of foster care is the provision of stability and safety for children who may have experienced chaos and uncertainty in their lives. Foster families offer a stable environment, often leading to improved emotional and psychological well-being for the child. In Northern Ireland, approximately 85% of children in foster care report feeling safe and secure in their foster placements, highlighting the effectiveness of this system in providing a protective environment.

Foster care offers children opportunities for personal and educational development that they might not have access to in their previous circumstances. Foster carers are often trained to support the educational needs of children, which can lead to improved academic outcomes. According to recent statistics, around 70% of children in foster care in Northern Ireland achieve academic progress during their placement, which is a significant improvement compared to their performance before entering the system.

Foster carers in Northern Ireland are supported by a network of social workers, therapists, and educational professionals. This multidisciplinary support system ensures that the child's needs are met comprehensively. Additionally, many foster carers form lasting bonds with the children they care for, providing a sense of family and belonging that can persist even after the child leaves the care system.

Despite the best efforts of the foster care system, placement instability remains a significant challenge. Frequent moves between foster homes can lead to further trauma and emotional distress for children. Statistics indicate that around 15% of children in foster care in Northern Ireland experience three or more placements within a year, which can disrupt their education and relationships and hinder their emotional recovery.

Northern Ireland faces a shortage of foster carers, which can result in children being placed in homes that may not fully meet their needs or in distant locations, separating them from their community and school. As of 2023, there is an estimated shortfall of 200 foster families, which places additional pressure on the existing carers and the system as a whole.

Many children entering foster care have experienced significant trauma, which can manifest in emotional and behavioural challenges. Foster carers often face difficulties in managing these issues, especially if they do not receive adequate support or training. While foster care provides a safety net, it is not a cure-all, and some children continue to struggle with the long-term effects of their early experiences. Reports suggest that about 30% of fostered children in Northern Ireland require specialised mental health support, highlighting a gap in the services provided.

I can only speak from my experience and knowledge of foster care. Despite this, I grew up in the same household as many other children over the years. We had very diverse experiences. This transition not only introduced me to a new family but also enveloped me in a tapestry of relationships— foster siblings, unrelated grandparents, aunts, uncles, and cousins, all weaving together the intricate threads of my newfound existence.

The tapestry of my past is adorned with vibrant hues of gratitude, especially during those enchanting moments spent on family holidays. These were the threads of joy that bound us together, creating cherished memories that continue to illuminate the fabric of my journey. The joys of going to a swimming club, brownies, guitar lessons, Irish dancing, and roller discos brought me profound enjoyment where I could excel and be myself. Aged 9, I took a massive fascination in Elvis Presley and with precision, I compiled two wonderful scrapbooks.

In reflecting upon the unknown paths that lay ahead, I can't help but acknowledge the profound impact foster care had on shaping the person I am today. It is a testament to the transformative power of love, resilience, and the unwavering belief that every individual deserves a chance to flourish against all odds. In foster care, the truth prevails: the vast majority of children find themselves there through no fault of their own. I, too, never asked to be thrust into the arms of the State. Yet, the misconceptions surrounding foster care persist, anchored in a misguided victim-blaming mentality. The prevailing narrative often suggests that we children were, somehow, at fault, that we somehow earned our place in this system. The reality, however, is far from it.

As foster children, we had to navigate turbulent waters caught in circumstances beyond our control. Regrettably, society all too often paints us with unwelcome labels, of danger, delinquency, or as damaged goods, side-lining the harrowing narratives of our early lives—lives all-too-often marred by trauma, abuse, and neglect, too easily forgotten.

When I found solace in the embrace of a foster family, I kept my story guarded, hesitant to unveil the uniqueness that set me apart. In the care system, I was reduced to mere digits—a number, a case, a file—struggling against the current of dehumanising bureaucracy. Society often throws shadows on the potential of those in foster care, predicting prison over university, mental health struggles over triumphs. While statistics lack the definitive evidence to support these claims, it's disheartening that foster children are over 5 times more likely than their peers in 'families of origin' to find trouble's doorstep, and I am using this term in its widest possible sense.

Reflecting on my journey, I harboured a constant fear of consequences, aware of society's expectations. Yet, within me, stirred a rebellious spirit, notably for the thrill of driving. Once, as I sped along a dual carriageway in my early twenties, the flashing lights of a police car pulled me over and shook me to my core. A stern warning and an imminent booking loomed, yet an unexpected twist of fate spared me that day as I received no penalties. Eventually, the inevitable did catch up with me, not once but twice, as the cold lens of a speed camera captured my moments of recklessness.

In my sight of blindness engrossed with settling into my new foster home I could not navigate the acceptance of being fostered, bringing me a lot more attention if I was not. Muddling through these treacherous deep waters brought on an array of stirred emotions deep inside of me, of shame, rejection and embarrassment caused by the very people who did not want me. Even the term 'foster child' is stigmatising in itself, setting me apart from other children. I despised question time when people would ask what my surname was, followed on by where I lived and who my mum and dad were. In the quite typical Northern Ireland mentality, people would press harder, having to know my family connections for their own pleasure but giving no reflection of the invasive manner they were subjecting me to. People pressed harder probably genuinely not knowing the displeasure they were causing me of wanting to dig deeper into my complicated arrangement to find out how many brothers and sisters I had. Did I resemble my mum or dad? The thought of having to explain myself in these circumstances where I would lie through my teeth but get caught out, anyway. Triggered by all the uncomfortable questioning, my body would tremble in fear, worried that people would know my secret. I would start overthinking and making up fictitious scenarios in my head, as if I was being judged by them, or that they felt only pity for me.

People's perceptions of me stirred my emotions, often leaving me fearful, disgusted, angry, and frustrated. It was never an option for me to show my vulnerability, as that was deemed a weakness. Instead, I showcased to society that I was happy and relatively stable. No help was ever offered to me to syphon through the layers of emotions, doubts, and rejections that I carried on my shoulders about being fostered. It was rooted deep inside me. I took everything to heart and internalised it. It was *my* problem and *my* responsibility to deal with it. Many people did not have the faintest idea why I was in care, nor was it their business. It was my secret and I was trying to keep it guarded as long as it was possible.

With my utter determination to fit into society, I was overshadowed by the mystical beliefs of what others perceived foster care to be. Sure, how would they stand a chance? Foster kids are 'bad' kids, there is a big possibility that they will turn out like their ma or da or how would they have any prospect of success? That just drove me further to blend into society and more determined to prove my worth rather than carrying this label and being a statistic.

Let me unveil a truth: children in foster care should not bear the responsibility of constantly having to 'prove their worth'. It is a societal lens that distorts reality, casting shadows on the potential, resilience, and untapped brilliance within each of us. My story, though shaped by a lifelong struggle for acceptance, is a testament to the indomitable spirit that refuses to be confined by the expectations of others. Then came people's judgments about foster children, based on misconceptions of who they thought I was, rather than taking the time to understand the real me. I desperately sought approval and recognition from others, relying on praise to prove my worth, to show that I wasn't a delinquent or a wicked child.

Pining to belong was my major struggle. Grateful for the opportunities that were provided to me and wanting for nothing as far as shelter, food, clothes, and materialistic stuff was concerned, I struggled to belong while in foster care. Where I once had an incredible bond with my foster mother, the dynamics of the family were continually changing because of social services sending more babies and children along with biological babies being born. The family was getting bigger, with mountains of babysitting and housework to be done. I just felt that I was being wedged out, not intentionally but just in my thoughts.

Prior to this I developed a bond with my foster parent's family, some who loved me unconditionally. I realised my position in the family was not what I thought. This was brought home to me on the death of my foster grandmother, who I visited from the age of 17 months, prior to being fostered. The picture at the front of my book was taken at her house when I was 3 years old with Lassie the dog. I was deeply affected by the death of my foster grandmother. I had built up a very close relationship with her. I went on holiday to Guernsey with her and spent weekends and summer holidays living in her house when I worked part time in my teens. However at my foster grandmother's funeral the priest read out her childrens' names and the number of grand-children. To my disbelief I was not included in that number. This confirmed that I didn't actually belong to the extended foster family. I tried to talk about my disappointment with other relatives of my foster grandmother, but I was brushed off and more or less dismissed. Those bonds with foster family members that were transfixed during my time in care became less and less when I left foster care, leaving a desperate feeling of emptiness and needing to belong.

Education

NERVOUS AND EXCITED, I joined Primary 3 in 1978, in the last term at a new Catholic Primary School run by nuns. A feeling of anticipation engulfed me on my first day, worried if I would fit in and integrate with the other children, closely protecting myself from the realms of my hidden secret of coming from a children's home and being a fostered child.

My school was different in that it was split across two sites, though it was amalgamated when I moved up to the next class. On the 27th of May 1978, I made my First Holy Communion, loving all the attention of people admiring me in my beautiful white dress.

I settled into school life, making new friends and attending birthday parties. Perhaps not the brightest in the class, yet my enthusiasm and zest for learning were infectious. Class tests were my biggest dread, being marked on my ability, not capability. I did something awful in one of those tests where I did not know the meaning of a word and stupidly wrote 'look it up in the dictionary.' How immature of me. I would be chastised for this and brought to the attention of the entire class. It brought me a lot of embarrassment but I learnt my lesson.

At school, I was an overactive child and found it incredibly difficult to sit at peace or be quiet for any length of time. To my dismay, one teacher took umbrage at this and sent me to the principal's office. My body shook in trepidation, fearing for my life. I was met by an angry nun who appeared to be taking out her distress on me, hitting me across my bare hand with a metre ruler. My hand was throbbing and ached with the pain. There was no way I was ever going back there.

One day, my sister's teacher sent for me to see her. In these unfamiliar situations, my body would tremble with trepidation, imagining that something horrific was going to happen to me. This teacher had instructed me to tell the class the eight times tables because my sister did not know them. So, there I was in front of the entire class, all gawking at me, fearing for my life over something trivial.

In the last two years at primary school, I was taught by an older, smartly dressed woman who would apply her lipstick many times during class. This woman was a snob and always looked down on me. She made me feel totally worthless and often asked me, 'Child dear, are you stupid?' Her 'put-downs' drove me the other way, making me more determined to show my worth and prove myself to people later in life. When at P7, we were asked to bring in money for the 'White Babies.' It was only years later that I learnt they were actually collecting for the White Babies at Nazareth Lodge, the children's home where I had lived for the first seven years of my life. How ironic was that?

After failing my eleven-plus (11+), an examination done in Northern Ireland in the last year of primary school to assess a pupil's ability in mathematics and English to gain entry into grammar schools, I started a Catholic High School run by more nuns. Scores from this test provided evidence of suitable academic streams at High School. I failed my eleven-plus because in my Early Years Foundation Stage, there was no one there to ensure that I learnt and developed well and gained the knowledge and skills to start school. No one ever supervised my homework or encouraged me when I lived in the children's home. To my disappointment, I only made it to the middle academic stream at High School.

High School was a more unfamiliar environment than primary school. It was an all-girls' school from all walks of life and backgrounds. In my first year, I won over my classmates where I was handpicked to be Class Captain. I found this to be an incredible achievement and it boosted my confidence. Initially, I appeared to be liked by all my peers until some girls found out I was fostered. I blamed this on the form teacher who was handing out parent's letters with their names on them. *My surname differed from that of my foster parents.*

With great trepidation, I would walk to the front of the class and receive my letter, wondering what people thought of me. I just felt the teacher could have been more diplomatic and discreet rather than singling me out. Nothing would have prepared me for the fierce bullying of being taunted for not living with my parents and being a fostered child. The name calling was awful. I despised having a different surname from my foster parents. Time and time again, I begged social services to change my surname to that of my foster parents. I was told it was not possible because I was fostered, not adopted. I felt everyone was against me and did not understand the turmoil I was experiencing. The bullying continued for many years at High School.

Thankfully, I was lucky to meet decent friends who accepted me for who I was and never broached the subject of me being fostered. I remain in touch with some of those friends today, which I am truly blessed to have.

So, through all my trials and tribulations, it turned out I was one of the brightest in my class. I had a great work ethic and was always eager to learn. But English language was my worst subject. I struggled massively with comprehension and writing stories, lacking creativity but, I was brilliant at spellings and reading. I convinced myself that I had missed out on the foundation stage of my life as a child and that is where my struggles came from. I was always asked to read in English class, which I took great pride in and was fantastic for my confidence. One day, my English teacher was calling out the class roll and called out my name, then looked up at me and asked if my mother had something against me at birth? To my horror, I replied 'no, sir' then he laughed and went on and on about calling your child 'Isobel.' Reeling from his reaction, I was disgusted that a man of his calibre had the audacity to make any judgement about me. He knew nothing about me and the hardships I had encountered of not having my mother in my life. It deeply disturbed me.

When I entered my new class to prepare me for my exams, I came across an outstanding accounts teacher who took a great interest in me for my ability and hunger for the subject. She knew nothing about me except that I had a great flair and passion for accounts. I soon realised this person was so inspiring, and felt she wanted the best for me. Her inspiration was like tonic and I thrived in her class, passing with flying colours. And indeed, she was the very person who I would look up to and carry this throughout my education.

What's in a Name?

Isobel

"What's in a name? That which we call a rose by any other name would smell just as sweet."
—William Shakespeare, *Romeo and Juliet.*

JUST BEFORE MY fourteenth birthday in 1985, I was given a fantastic opportunity to go to France on a French exchange. Organised by my French teacher to improve my French, I had been matched with a pen pal a few months prior, with whom I had been corresponding. Having never been abroad before, social services were adamant that I go, applying for my new passport. I was delighted to be handed my new passport. Skipping down to the bedroom and sitting on the edge of the bed, I was bursting to see my new document that I possessed. I stumbled across the incorrect spelling of my name, reading *Isabel*, with trepidation. How could this be? Trying to make sense of this in my head, I reasoned with myself that it must be correct. From childhood, I was told my name was spelt *Isobel*. A name that I loved and cherished, making it even more significant as it was handpicked by both or either of my parents. Then to find out years later that both my biological grandmother and great-grandmother were called *Isobella*. My name gave me my identity and some sort of attachment to a family I was estranged from.

Her Majesty's British Passport that I received had receipt of my birth certificate, and there was no chance they would make such a big mistake. I never had the courage to tell anyone, so I just kept it a secret. It niggled my mind as I was so desperate to take ownership of this awful mistake. Taking matters into my own hands, I slowly started changing the spelling of my name to *Isabel* in my daily life. I wasn't brave enough in my teenage years to change my name on doctor records, school, or dentist in case I was questioned and had to explain. All my examination certificates from school were in the name of Isobel.

The repercussions of this incorrect spelling of my name would carry with me well into my adulthood, having to continually say to doctors, nurses, dentists, receptionists 'You've my name spelt incorrectly,' without offering any explanation.

Leaving no stone unturned in my forties, I wrote to the Sisters of Nazareth to investigate why my name was misspelt. In a handwritten letter, it stated:

It must have been distressing to find the variation in forenames Isabel/Isobel. Again, I'm afraid this is a constant problem for us using the archives. I suspect often children were received without written paperwork accompanying them. Perhaps being 'handed over' by someone unrelated to the child who could only give the name verbally, resulting in phonetic recording.

It appears my parents never picked up the correct spelling of my name when they received a Parental Rights Order from the court to legally hand me over to the State, or worse perhaps, they simply did not care.

No one ever took the time to check the spelling of my name, even though many must have found it unusual. Someone from the Sisters of Nazareth made a horrendous mistake. A mistake that I would carry throughout my life, still having to pick up their mess during my adulthood.

Spreading My Wings

AGED NINETEEN, I WENT to Guernsey for the summer to work. I had been there as a teenager on holiday. Going solo, I took two flights and eventually arrived on the island without accommodation or a job. After one night in a bed-and-breakfast, I ventured on a bus with my luggage and tent to the unknown to find a campsite. There, I was disappointed to be told they were fully booked. So, I trekked on foot for miles to another campsite to be told the same thing again. In my moment of distress, I cried hard, and the proprietor took pity on me, welcoming me with open arms.

Never having put up a tent before, I reeled in people to help in my time of need. After a day of tireless walking and visiting many hotels, I secured a summer job as a server, chambermaid and bartender.

Knackered and dishevelled from the summer heat as I returned to the campsite, I was met by the caretaker, who was busy repairing a bike to sell. How pleased I was to see him and excitedly told him I would be its rightful owner. My new pink bike became my means of transport around the island, taking me to work and my many adventures.

Every morning I set off on my bike to the hotel about five miles away. I served breakfast, changed beds and cleaned rooms to then escape for a few hours to enjoy the summer heat. I returned in the evening to serve dinner to the residents and drinks in the bar, sometimes until ridiculous hours of the night.

I was working six days per week, spending my day off taking boat trips to visit the islands of Herm and Sark and cycling around Guernsey. Once a week, my treat was at the local hairdressers, where I got my hair in a French plait.

Two weeks after pitching my tent, the owner moved the workers to an unused hilly field in the camp. There I met young people from all backgrounds and walks of life, sharing their stories and experiences, while we cooked our food over the campfire. I was living life to the fullest, unaware that the survival skills I had learned as a child were strengthening me as a person.

After my ten-week working holiday in Guernsey, I caught the travel bug. Over the next few years, I went on holidays to Magaluf and Santa Ponsa in Majorca and Cyprus. I also took a last-minute cruise to Egypt and Israel, where I rode a camel to the Pyramids and even got to go inside one. I also visited Jerusalem to see the Wailing Wall, Jesus' birthplace, and the site of his crucifixion.

Higher Education

AFTER ONLY PASSING TWO CSEs (equivalent to 'O' Levels) I returned to school to re-sit my exams that had changed to GCSEs. I only passed a further two exams, which were not enough to sit my 'A' Levels. I had no option but to leave High School and go on to further education at the local technical college.

Moving into further education was a shock to my system after coming from an all-girls Catholic school. People at the technical college came from all walks of life and ages. I felt grateful as some of my friends had also followed me on to the same course. Nobody really cared where you came from. At last, the bullying stopped and people just accepted me as another person.

It was my accounts teacher at school who inspired me to pursue my education in Business and Finance. Due to not having sufficient exams I went on to do a BTEC First Award (equivalent to five GCSEs), which led onto doing a BTEC National (equivalent to 3 'A' levels).

At Tech, I came across another accounts teacher who knew nothing about me. She was so passionate about the subject, often telling me "Wee buns.", which meant easy peasy in her language. I was so inspired by her and I had many a laugh in her class. After all the struggles and obstacles I encountered of failing my exams at school, I had turned it around and successfully passed all my exams at technical college.

The inspiration from both my accounts teachers gave me the confidence and courage to apply to university in England, where I got accepted to do a Higher National Diploma in Business and Finance. Having that inspiration was instrumental in my believing in myself and my capabilities, irrespective of what my primary school teacher thought of me all those years. That could have marred my life, but I turned it into a positive and believed that with hard work and sheer dedication, I could improve my prospects. I loved everything about university life and met some incredible people who remain friends with me to this day. I excelled in my HND, earning mainly distinctions, which paved the way for me to pursue a BA (Hons) in Business Administration. My degree took me to a different level and tested me academically, although I often doubted myself. With all the tears I shed and late nights, my hard work paid off as I successfully passed my degree and achieved a 2:1. When I returned home, social services asked me to participate in a promotional campaign on fostering. I was now 23, more mature, and had accepted in my heart that I was fostered. I did not really care what people thought of me anymore. Preparing my script for BBC radio and television, I was told that I was the FIRST foster child in Northern Ireland to have gone to university and achieved a degree in the Down and Lisburn Trust. Bursting with pride of my achievement, I was no longer a statistic, a faceless name on a file, I had proved my worth and no longer felt I had to prove myself to anyone but myself.

Having bagged my degree I had the urge to return to night class at my local further education college to re-sit my GCSE Mathematics and English Language exams that I had repeatedly failed. I was determined to achieve at least a C. On my fifth attempt, I passed English Language with a B, and on my third attempt, I passed Mathematics with a C.

Life After Care

READY OR NOT, I left foster care in July 1994 aged 23, two weeks after returning from university. I experienced my second 'desertion'; this time from the State. As a care leaver, I was offered no help and support with my transition from care to independent living. In fact, I do not think anyone was ever informed of my leaving. Nowadays, it is the duties of the health and social care trusts in Northern Ireland to assess and meet care leavers individual needs and provide support to improve their life prospects as they make the transition to independent living. This is up to the age of 21 or beyond if in education. Care leavers are now provided with a leaving care grant to help purchase essentials for moving into their new home. I only wished that help was available to me when I moved out of care all those years ago. I was simply a name on a file, a statistic, really no one cared.

The Children (Northern Ireland) Order 1995 marked the province's first major change in child care legislation for almost thirty years.[1] This was amended by the Children (Leaving Care) Act (NI) 2002. The Department of Health, Social Services, and Public Safety set out a legal framework which affected young people aged 18 to 21 who have been either eligible or relevant children, or both. If at the age of 21, the young person is still being helped by the responsible HSS Trust with education or training, they remain a former relevant child to the end of the agreed programme of education or training, even if that takes them past the age of 21.

The Act also emphasised the importance of preparing young people for leaving care. It is crucial that HSS Trusts ensure those in their care are adequately prepared for the transition and have access to support when they leave. Young

---

[1] www.health-ni.gov.uk

people approaching the time when they will leave care, do so from a wide variety of backgrounds and circumstances, at various ages, and with differing levels of support available to them from family and friends. A flexible service is, therefore, required to meet the wide range of potentially differing experiences and needs of young people. The quality of preparation for leaving care, and the aftercare provided, will profoundly impact the successful transition of a young person to independent living and potentially influence the quality of the rest of their life. Many young people leaving care, particularly those who are required to live independently, can face very severe financial difficulties, both immediately and during their transition to full independence. It should be borne in mind that the HSS Trust's duty to provide assistance to former relevant children extends until the young person reaches the age of 21. If a young person has no parent to turn to for help, or where a parent does not have the capacity to provide assistance, it is to be expected that the young person will turn to the responsible HSS Trust for help and support.

Whilst it should have been an exciting time in my life, with hopes, dreams and aspirations like any young person, instead I struggled to navigate through treacherous waters to find somewhere to live and very little money in my bank account. My summer job was finishing in a matter of weeks and I had a small overdraft incurred from university due to be paid back almost immediately. I was reluctant to put my burden onto others, too ashamed and embarrassed to show any vulnerability and weakness, in case I would be judged or looked down on. I had built a steel wall around me to shield my struggles and put on a brave face to the preying eye I was coping and managing well. Despite my woes, I had incredible energy, drive, and motivation and always held onto hope that I could turn my situation around and things would get better.

Braving the storm, on my own I moved all my belongings in black bin bags and a holdall in my beat-up chocolate mini into my rented home that I found. It was my first car, for which I had scraped one-hundred and fifty pounds together. My foster parents kindly paid for my car insurance. I often thought was that maybe my leaving care grant but it was never mentioned.

The sheer absence of not belonging and having a connection to a real family was more evident when I moved out of foster care. Through no fault of my own, I found myself very much on my own, lonely, and longing to belong to a real family. I had conjured it up in my head what a real family should be like comparing it to that of my friends and people I met. I was fortunate to have great supportive friends, but my life was nothing like the life they came from with a supportive and wide network of family. They were absorbed in family life, doing things together and watching out for one another. Even a simple family photograph displayed on the walls of a home, family gatherings or people pouring their heart out how wonderful their family is, triggered me as I never got to experience that with my real family. I never had that. At times I craved for that sort of life, it was an incredible loss. Through passing time, I slowly started to accept my situation, but the loss never really went away until I had my own family. I was never envious of my friends, but I yearned to have what they had. My friend's families welcomed me with open arms as I was their child. Sometimes, I felt I was imposing when they offered me to stay for dinner, stay over or whatever. I carried a lot of guilt because of my situation and never wanted them to feel pity for me. If only I was brave enough to speak up then about how I was really feeling instead of carrying all that guilt. All these years, I have never forgotten their kindness and was eternally grateful for what they did for me.

After my summer job, I was fortunate to secure a temporary office clerk position in the neighbouring town. By that time, I had paid off my university debt but was barely surviving financially. I was buying my clothes in charity shops and collecting coupons to reduce my food bill. I was simply robbing Peter to pay Paul. It never entered my head to stop working and rely on benefits. I was determined to work and better myself. Then, thrust upon me, I was forced to find another home to live. That threw my life into disarray. The feeling of having nowhere to live is the most horrible feeling in the world. It caused me significant anxiety and worry, with the added pressure of moving and the financial burden it brought.

I found a one bedroom run-down flat with no luxury trimmings such as heating and a washing machine. It was my last resort and I was so grateful to get a roof over my head. I had taken out a loan to buy a new washing machine paying ridiculous interest, but I had no other option. Just as I got myself sorted; I faced another major obstacle. The business where I was working had been sold to a property developer. I was going to be unemployed within a matter of weeks. I threw myself into another tranche of job applications, receiving more rejections, then to be finally offered a job interview. I was elated when I made it through the gruelling interview to be offered the job as a receptionist at the local museum. It was not what I wanted to do, but I had bills to pay and had to financially survive. The new job opened another door for me, securing a casual receptionist post at the local arts centre alongside my full-time post.

Then unexpectedly, I met a wonderful lady at work looking for someone to run her bed and breakfast while she was on holidays. I jumped at the chance and before I knew it, I was juggling all these jobs. My unwavering determination and zest to do well was finally paying off. My beat-up mini car had run its course and I bought my next car. A second-hand Peugeot 205 from a girl at work for one-thousand pounds, taking a loan to finance it.

Alongside my full-time job in February 1997, I needed to supplement my income. I started a Kleeneze business distributing catalogues of household items and cleaning products to people's houses. It was extremely hard work especially in the wet and dark evenings but I persevered and built up a reputable business. I expanded my business recruiting other people, working below me, creaming off a percentage of their sales. At last, I could see the fruits of my labour. Initially, only a quick way to make money, I ended up running my part time business for five years alongside working full time.

I was hungry to get a promotion and better myself and applied for a job in Belfast. After an intense interview I secured the job as Visitor Co-ordinator at Queen's University of Belfast in April 1997. I was delighted to learn that, out of ninety applicants, I had secured the position. At Queen's University of Belfast, I loved the camaraderie of meeting new people from all walks of life and putting my skills and knowledge to good use, taking people on guided tours around the university and organising and displaying different exhibitions. I came up with the idea of organising The Big School exhibition engaging with schools across Northern Ireland to participate in an art competition that would later be exhibited with artefacts from the past from the local museum, inviting guests to the opening. It was a major success.

The One and Only

AS A YOUNG CHILD, I often went to the country, to visit or stay with my foster-grandparents. I thoroughly enjoyed the drive, admiring all the beautiful houses and well-kept gardens. There was one particular house that I always made a point of looking at, a beautiful big bungalow up a driveway with an immaculate garden full of colourful flowers, shrubs and rockery. This person kept it meticulous and it was a joy to see.

On the 6th October 1983, two Protestant members of the Royal Ulster Constabulary, now the Police Service of Northern Ireland, were shot and killed while on foot patrol where we had lived in town. By the following April, 1984, aged 13, we had moved house to live in the rural area in the country. To my surprise, our new house was directly across the road from that beautiful bungalow I had admired as a child all those years ago.

Just as we were settling in, our neighbour Roy from that bungalow, arrived down to the house to introduce himself. I never really paid much attention to him as he was older and I had nothing in common with him.

Settling into country life took a lot of time to get used to. Where I once played with my neighbours on the street, greens or play park, my life resorted to sometimes playing in the garden with the other kids in the house. It wasn't the same, so I joined the local youth club in the country meeting new friends, of a similar age to myself. And before I knew it, I had been welcomed in by the locals meeting up with them now and again. This opened a wider network of friends and the older ones were driving me about most weekends, going to different places.

In this circle of friends, I was introduced to a fella who later became my boyfriend. I was 14 then. We only met on the weekends. My friends from high school would often join this group of friends from the country and we started going to discos. Roy, my neighbour, was in this circle of friends and even though I saw him, our paths never really crossed until one day

I asked him for a lift to the city. I knew Roy was travelling there most days to study. I had tracked down a fella from the children's home and really wanted to meet him. I went with my friend from school. That was the first time I really spoke to Roy, and he was actually hilarious and enjoyable to be around.

When I was out with my friends and if Roy was about, I always made sure I chatted to him. He then gave me lifts with other friends to different places and to my part-time shop assistant job that was eight miles away. I was offered a babysitting job some weekends and mentioned this to Roy, and before I knew it, he would pop round to see me. I was still going out with my then boyfriend at the time, but it was nothing serious, and I rarely saw him as I was too occupied with working every weekend. Roy and I became good friends, and I really enjoyed his company. He made me laugh loads. He was the first person in my life to show a genuine interest in me and give me advice when needed. One Saturday afternoon, I had met my boyfriend halfway up the road from where I lived. I wasn't overly happy with him as I had felt we had nothing really in common, so I ended the relationship. On my walk back home, Roy was driving past and stopped to give me a lift. When I got into the car, I had a right wee giggle, telling him I had finished with my boyfriend. I also mentioned I was invited to a 25th anniversary party that evening and was going solo. To my astonishment, he invited himself to the party.

Over the next four months, I met Roy now and again as friends. We started walking and going to badminton together. They were really happy times. My sister invited him to her 18th birthday party, and I never left his side all evening, laughing and joking. It turned out we actually had so much in common. Then, before he left, he asked me to go out with him. I wanted to tell him yes but, in my heart, I felt that I needed permission from my foster mother because Roy was seven years older than me and was also a Protestant. I did not know how she would react to the situation. So, I laughed at his request, telling him when I got back from my ten day school holiday in Spain, I would let him know.

Seven months after my 16th birthday in 1987, Roy and I started dating. A month later, on the 22nd of November, we both went on a proper date to my school formal at the Thrupenny Bit at the King's Hall, Belfast. I wore a dire pink bridesmaid dress I borrowed. We danced all night, and my friend Joanne entertained the crowd singing Livin' on a Prayer by Bon Jovi. It was one of the best nights I ever had. In such a short time, our relationship got serious, meeting each other almost every night and at weekends.

Before I met Roy, I had no real interests. He introduced me to walking - mostly across fields, woods and forests, often in a pair of wellington boots I borrowed from him. He was a fanatic cyclist, and before I knew it, he had me on my rusty bike with squeaky wheels, cycling for hours on roads that I had never been on. I was so unfit and yapped so much that I was tired, but he just turned a blind eye. I persevered because I loved and enjoyed being in his company. Roy's desire to get me to cycle regularly was fulfilled when he took me to select my own racer bike for my 17th birthday in March 1988. The prices of the bikes he was looking at were astronomical, but he insisted on getting me a top-range bike. So, I picked a range racer MBK, a blue one, my favourite colour. My bike became my pride and joy, where both of us cycled for miles, enjoying the freedom of the country roads and each other's company.

Our first big adventure with our bikes was on holidays together in July 1988, aged 17 in Wales where we drove by car with our bikes on the roof rack. Arriving exhausted in the middle of that night at Holyhead, we pitched our tent in the first green area we saw. No sooner after falling asleep we were wakened by a security guard to remove our tent. We had pitched our tent at some industrial estate where people were going to their work, gawking at us. We had a right wee giggle. So off we went on our travels, staying at a campsite at Llandudno and Rhyl, enjoying every moment on our bikes in the warm summer heat. Then disaster struck. Roy had entered a car park and we heard an almighty thud. We had not realised there was a height restriction on the entrance, and sadly my new bike was mangled. I was absolutely devastated, but Roy reassured me he would get me a new bike on my return. We tried not to let this disrupt our plans, so we travelled down to Wolverhampton, stopping over at my foster mum's family and then heading to London to stay with Roy's sister. It was one of the best holidays I ever had. Over the years, we returned to Wales several times enjoying brief breaks, those times, without the bikes!

On my 17th birthday, I took my first driving lesson with a driving instructor. Roy, in his kind nature, took me for additional lessons in his car to give me as much experience as possible being out on the roads. On a wet, dreary day on November 10th 1988, I nervously took my driving test and passed. Roy rewarded me by insuring me on his car.

Hitting The Self-Destruct Button

I STRUGGLED MASSIVELY WITH jealousy, insecurity and trust issues with my relationship with Roy. I knew in my heart that it had manifested from the trauma and abandonment I endured as a child, but did not comprehend how to navigate out of the turmoil.

Relationships, whether romantic or platonic, are built on pillars of trust, security, and emotional intimacy. However, these fundamental elements can be compromised for individuals who have grown up in state care, without the natural dynamics of a family of origin. When someone has not experienced stable family bonds during their formative years, feelings of jealousy, insecurity, and trust issues often become deeply rooted in their adult relationships. Understanding the origins of these emotional challenges is essential for fostering healthier relationships and is something I have spent a lifetime doing.

The family of origin is typically where individuals first learn how to form and maintain emotional connections. From infancy, a child in a stable family setting experiences attachment—a bond formed through love, care, and consistent emotional availability from caregivers. These early attachments play a pivotal role in shaping how a person perceives love, trust, and emotional safety later in life.

According to *attachment theory*, formulated by John Bowlby, secure attachments in childhood foster confidence and emotional resilience in adulthood. When these bonds are missing or inconsistent, as is often the case for children in foster care or state institutions, insecure attachment styles can develop. These insecure attachments may manifest as:

Anxious attachment, characterised by a deep fear of abandonment and constant worry about whether others love them.

Avoidant attachment, where individuals protect themselves by avoiding close emotional relationships, often due to a fear of rejection.

Without the consistent presence of caregivers who provide emotional security, many children in care struggle to form healthy attachments, leading to relational difficulties later in life. Children in the care of the state—whether through foster homes, group homes, or other forms of institutional care—are often subject to frequent moves, inconsistent caregiving, and, in some cases, neglect or abuse. These experiences can result in a lack of emotional attunement. In a family of origin, caregivers often understand and respond to a child's emotional needs. In contrast, children in state care may not receive the individualised attention required to foster emotional development. This lack of emotional attunement can lead to feelings of being unloved or unwanted, forming a foundation for insecurity.

They can also lead to a sense of chronic instability. Frequent changes in living situations, caregivers, or schools are common for children in the care system. This constant upheaval can create a sense of impermanence, making it difficult for individuals to feel secure in relationships later in life. They may expect abandonment or believe that emotional closeness is fleeting.

Additionally, trauma and loss are commonplace. Many children enter the care system after experiencing trauma, whether due to neglect, abuse, or the loss of parents. These early traumas can compound feelings of mistrust and insecurity, leading to emotional defence mechanisms like jealousy or hypervigilance in relationships.

For individuals who did not experience the security of a family of origin, adult relationships can be fraught with emotional challenges. The absence of early emotional stability often leads to feelings of jealousy. A common response to perceived threats in a relationship, jealousy can stem from deep-seated fears of abandonment. For someone who has experienced inconsistent caregiving, any perceived challenge to a relationship, such as a partner's friendship with another person, can trigger feelings of inadequacy or fear that they will be replaced. Also, insecurity is not uncommon. Without early experiences of unconditional love and acceptance, it can be difficult for individuals to believe they are worthy of love. They may constantly seek validation or reassurance from their partner, leading to clingy or dependent behaviours. The fear that they are not "good enough" can undermine their sense of self-worth, making it difficult to trust in their partner's affection. Lastly, trust issues tend to manifest. Typically, trust is built through consistent, positive interactions over time. However, people who grew up in care may have experienced betrayal, neglect, or abuse, all of which erode their ability to trust others. Even in a healthy relationship, they may struggle with suspicions, fear of betrayal, or difficulty relying on their partner.

Roy was the first person I ever loved and who loved me, but I just did not know how to deal with the relationship. It felt like I was constantly hitting the self-destruct button, ruining everything in my power and making us both miserable with the petty arguments that I always started. Roy had had enough and could not handle it anymore. Just after my 19th birthday, Roy ended the relationship. I was distraught. I took myself to Guernsey for the summer to work to get away from the heartache and distract my mind.

Early in the morning before I caught my flight to Guernsey, I took myself up to Roy's car to get my cheque book. To my surprise, Roy came out of the back door towards me and handed me an envelope, instructing me not to open it until I got on the flight. We both kissed and hugged each other and said an emotional farewell. I loved this guy, and the chemistry we had was like nothing I had ever experienced before.

Sitting on my first flight to East Midlands, I nervously opened Roy's envelope. Inside was a cassette tape he had made of my favourite songs and a poem he had written. In those days, I listened to my music on a battery-operated Walkman, a portable music cassette with earphones. Tears flooded down my cheeks. I so wanted this guy but was too caught up with my own insecurities and jealousy that it was not healthy for the both of us. All I could think was that he deserved better than me, and my self-worth was at rock bottom.

Two days after arriving in Guernsey I phoned Roy from a telephone box. He told me he would be out to visit me. I was so delighted. Being reunited with him was magical and I was so happy. We spent two joyous weeks together, driving around the island, going out to the pubs and sunbathing on the beach. We gave the relationship another chance and got back together.

Roy's natural influence radiated through me at different stages in our relationship. He could always see the goodness in me and wanted the best for me, sometimes more than I could see myself. I was hungry to do well, mainly having to prove myself to others being that child grown up in care. But Roy was different. He saw my potential and, with gentle prodding and valuable advice, opportunities opened for me I imagined would never happen.

He was the very person to encourage me to go to university. Even that reassurance in itself was invaluable. I started to believe in myself more and realised that I could achieve a lot more than I give myself credit for. His quest for me to do well was clear in all his actions. He took time out of his busy schedule to take me to university in England. I spent most evenings queuing up at the telephone boxes on campus with my ten pence coins that I gathered to hear his voice and catch up on the gossip. He surprised me with his endless talents, writing me poems in the early stages of our relationship. I missed him dreadfully while in England, but he visited me usually for a month at a time, bringing his bike to ride the canals. We had amazing times taking the train to London to see his sister and travelling to other places in the West Midlands. When I came home from university just after my 21st birthday in 1992, Roy proposed and we got engaged.

My jealousy, insecurities, and trust issues continued irrespective of getting engaged. It became unbearable and took its toll on the relationship. After having spent six years of dating on and off, Roy called off the engagement and ended the relationship for good in October 1993. I felt a total failure and was worried about what other people would say. I was absolutely devastated, and it broke my heart. Life without Roy was unbearable. I rang him a few times when I was in England, but he was not interested. I started to date a few other fellas, but they were nothing compared to the relationship I had with Roy.

Marrying My Best Friend

THEN, OUT OF THE BLUE, Roy rang my house phone while I was in my final year at university to check in with me to see how things were. I was in a better head space by then and had worked through my doubts, fears, and insecurities. As I was nearing the end of university, he wanted to come over, spend a week in Wales with me after my final exams, and then fly home together. I was very excited, as I really loved Roy and desperately wanted the relationship to work. The break had done us the power of good and we both realised that although sometimes it was difficult to be together, it was, in fact, more difficult to be apart.

While sitting at Birmingham airport, waiting for my last flight home from university, Roy gave me a few words of wisdom. He told me how incredibly proud he was of me, that I had so much potential, that the world was my oyster, and I could achieve anything. Talk about boosting me up. It was an incredible moment, as I knew in my heart how far I had come and all the tears I shed to get my degree. I felt his positivity and energy and I was so excited to embark on our next journey together when I returned to Northern Ireland.

On New Year's 1996, we went out to a disco to celebrate. Smooching over a slow dance on the floor, some mad guy randomly pushed Roy to the floor and knocked him out. An ambulance was called and took him to the hospital to get him checked over. The following morning, Roy asked me to marry him. It was such an emotional day as our relationship had come so far, and after nearly ten years of dating on and off, I was shocked when he proposed. Though Roy would tell you it was the bump to the head that sent him into a silly moment. I was absolutely ecstatic, as I loved Roy so much and really wanted to spend the rest of my life with him. He had shared the last ten years on and off with me through good times and bad times and was a massive part of my life. He really got and understood me, and we had this amazing chemistry that bound us together.

Everything that I had dreamt of all those years ago of being together had now come to reality. I was hopeful about my future.

On the 6th of November 1997, Roy and I got married in Barbados. It was an idyllic day; we took a helicopter ride around the island and then a limousine to a romantic meal by the sea. No one could take away my smile or happiness. He was the one and only!

After returning from honeymoon as a married couple, I had just opened up the door when Roy scooped me up and carried me over the threshold, entering our new home for the first time as Mr & Mrs Kelly.

Over the years, Roy has been my absolute rock. His inspiration, encouragement and influences have been never ending, always wanting the best for me and more. I believe this has played a massive part in my life, helping me to feel secure in myself, feel a sense of belonging to a family, and be the woman I am today. He has taught me about the simple things in life, like spending quality time together such as walking and riding our bikes, and not being extravagant. Thank goodness I have never been materialistic in any shape or form. His calmness and quiet demeanour have been quite the icing on the cake for me, often deescalating a situation or scenario I have found myself to be in. He has always been there and is the only person I can offload to, and makes no judgement. He accepts and appreciates who I am as a person. That has meant a lot to me as I can be myself when I am around him.

On November 6th 2022, Roy and I celebrated our 25th wedding anniversary. We invited family and friends to celebrate with us at the Slieve Donard Hotel in Newcastle. My friend Joanne who surprised us with a fancy car all those years at our blessing surprised us with a 25th anniversary cake. She is an incredible best friend to have, and I love her dearly.

A Home from Home

IN 1997, ROY AND I decided to buy our first home together in the country. It was a labourer's cottage with a quarter of an acre of garden, situated on a hill with the most fascinating views, overlooking the Mourne Mountains.

The word *home* is universally associated with warmth, safety, and belonging. For many, it evokes images of family gatherings, childhood bedrooms, and the feeling of security that comes from a stable family environment. But for those of us who have been raised, for a time, in the care of the state, where the natural dynamics of a family of origin are absent, the concept of home can be far more complex and elusive. The traditional understanding of home is more than just a physical space.

Home is a psychological and emotional concept tied to feelings of security, belonging, and identity. According to the geographer, Yi-Fu Tuan, *home* is a place imbued with emotional significance, where one feels safe and accepted. It is a key component in shaping one's self-identity and worldview. But when children grow up in care, without the continuity of a single home or a stable family structure, the meaning of home can become fragmented or even lost.

For individuals raised in state care, the search for a homeplace is often a journey of self-discovery. It's about finding or creating spaces—whether physical or emotional—where they can feel safe, validated, and whole. This may come later in life as they form relationships, find stability, or build their own families. This was true for me.

When sorting out the mortgage application, the financial advisor asked if any of us had a loan, as we therefore would not be eligible to get a mortgage. I was quaking in my boots because I had an outstanding loan for my latest car, which I hadn't mentioned at the meeting. When I got outside, I informed Roy that I had blown our chances of buying our first home together because of my outstanding debt. I was actually shaking as I told him, remembering how I used to be punished for doing something wrong when I lived in the children's home. I was actually reverting back to my childhood fears, imagining and building up a worst-case scenario that he would go berserk. He wasn't perturbed in the slightest and told me he would pay off the loan the next day. I was so taken aback by his generosity because no one in my life had shown me any type of kindness the way he did that day. Roy had also insisted that I change my car to a reliable motor, especially with all the driving to Belfast. I upgraded my car to a Renault 5, taking out a much bigger loan than I had expected.

In July 1997, we received the keys to our first home. It was such an exciting time. We had decided not to move in together until we were married, so I moved into the house myself. I had been cooped up on a second-floor flat for almost two years by then with no outdoor space or heating. The freedom of moving to a detached house with a garden and the nicest view was breath-taking. I was on cloud nine.

When I moved in on my own, I had an obsession with washing all my clothes and getting them aired outdoors on the humongous clothes line. I hadn't that freedom for such a long time, resorting to drying clothes in front of a Superser, in a damp flat. The outdoors and the fresh air brought so much joy to my bones.

Moving into our own house meant so much to me. I was tired of moving about and not having a base. I needed a place where I could belong, and call 'home'.

Work, Pregnancy and Me

THE TIME HAD COME when I was ready to leave my job at Queen's University of Belfast to better my prospects. In February 1999, I found a job close to where I lived as a Project Coordinator for an arts charity. Initially part-time, the job gradually crept up to full-time hours because of my success in growing the charity. After five years post-graduation, I was finally putting my degree to good use. My key role was to secure funding and produce an array of arts programmes for families, children, young people, adults, and older adults across the council areas, delivered by a team of artists. I felt I was born to lead this charity, with my aptitude for business and creativity. Beyond my wildest dreams, I had developed the charity and set up two social enterprises— an arts resource centre and a consultancy service in grant writing. I was successfully managing a small team of staff, and the charity was well known across the council area.

In 1999, I mentioned to Roy that I wanted to visit my university friend who had emigrated to Australia. Roy had other plans, as he wanted to start a family. From a very young age, I had always wanted to be a mummy so, that took precedence over everything, including the Australia trip. I was anxious about getting postnatal depression, ingrained in my brain because of my mother's struggles. I first visited my GP to discuss the possibilities. She reassured me it was not heredity and gave me folic acid. A few months later, I was pregnant with our first baby. Our first baby was due in April. I had always wanted a spring baby as it was my favourite season. We were both elated and booked a holiday to Portugal to celebrate our wonderful news. It was such an exciting time.

A few weeks before our holiday, I had some complications with the pregnancy, so we went to the local hospital in the evening. I was kept in overnight. The next day, the consultant, along with a nurse, scanned me, where I sadly discovered that our baby had died. We were both absolutely devastated. Rather than sending me to theatre, they kept me in for a further two days to pass the baby. It was a very painful time for the both of us. During this whole ordeal, I really missed having a mother to comfort and guide me through my pain. We had made so many plans in our heads about our new baby, and readjusting and dealing with the loss took considerable time. Someone had suggested planting a shrub in the garden and watching it grow with time. Twenty-four years later the shrub has grown immensely and blooms every year. Our two-week holiday to Portugal was a pretty sombre one. I always held out for hope that we would have a baby someday. On our 2nd wedding anniversary, I found out I was pregnant again. Around that time, I discovered I had negative blood type after a routine blood test. Most people have positive blood type. I often wondered which of my parents I inherited my blood type from. Ten days over my due date our bundle of joy arrived, our beautiful daughter Tierna. She was perfect and gorgeous in every way. I had always wanted a daughter and was so excited. She was our life and everything revolved around her. When she was born, Roy's mother insisted on staying over for the first few nights to do the night feeds. I was also fortunate to receive a fantastic nine-month maternity package from work, allowing me to work a set number of hours per week before returning full-time.

My foster mother provided us with some help when Tierna was a baby, looking after her one day per week when I returned back to work, but after a while it filtered out. Having to leave her with a childminder full-time broke my heart. When Tierna went to nursery school, she learned all the nursery rhymes. As a child, nursery rhymes are something we all learn, reiterated in our young brains, that we carry throughout our lives. To my embarrassment, I did not know them. I bought myself a nursery rhyme book and taught myself so we could both say them together at home.

A year passed, and we planned to extend our family. We were over the moon when I got pregnant with our second child. We were so looking forward to Tierna having a brother or sister. But sadly, at the early stages of that pregnancy, I had a second miscarriage. We both found it so difficult to process, dealing with the sudden loss and emptiness. It was an incredibly sad time. I held out hope and after eleven months, our beautiful son Ross came into the world. We were both elated. Mind you, Tierna wasn't, and asked us to take him back to where he came from.

Charity Life

ALONGSIDE MY FULL-TIME job and juggling two children, I set up a local charity, Ballee and District Community Group, in 2005 in the rural area where I lived. I called a public meeting to get local people involved. The response was phenomenal, with people from all walks of life eager to join the committee to better the lives of the wider community. For sixteen years, I held the post of chairperson in a voluntary capacity. I put my skills to good use applying for funding and organising different events and projects for local children, young people, adults and older people. We organised summer schemes, a cookery school, yoga, outdoor adventure activities, arts and crafts, outdoor play, flower arranging, trips, hanging baskets, circuits, a walking club, performances, BBQs, and afternoon tea. All of these events were held at Ballee Non-Subscribing Presbyterian Church Hall. Due to the charity's success, we enforced a five-mile radius policy to ensure we met the needs of local people. It was such a joyful and exciting time, and I met so many wonderful people who I became friends with. When Covid-19 arrived in 2020, I decided my role had come to an end and handed it over to the committee. None of the committee was interested in running the charity, so we decided to close down the charity.

In 2005, I had really wanted to extend my family. Ross and Tierna were three and five years old by then and it seemed the best time. Fortunately, I became pregnant quickly, and we were delighted. Things were going well and we were busy working full time and juggling two children. Then, just before I reached twelve weeks, I started to have complications and began feeling unwell. I rested up thinking it would pass, but sadly, the inevitable happened, and we had a third miscarriage. This time I had to go to theatre and the upheaval getting me there was a nightmare because of the bad snow at that time.

Just before going into theatre, the nurse discussed with us if we wanted to take the baby home to bury it. We were never asked that before, and it deeply disturbed me. My emotions were all over the place, and I kept crying. Roy asked if it was possible for the baby to go for medical research, and we both agreed. Two days before Christmas Day, 2005, I walked out of hospital broken and in despair. It was an incredibly difficult time getting through Christmas, but we did it. Almost ten months later, our beautiful second son, Craig, was born. It was such a joyful time. Craig is now 18 and is working as an apprentice travel consultant for Hays Travel. He decided that studying 'A' levels was not for him. I am so proud of what he has achieved and am looking forward to booking my holidays with him!

Records and Me

AFTER HAVING BEEN OUT of care for a long time, I became interested in locating my records. In February 2006, I wrote to South and East Belfast Trust, now known as Belfast Health and Social Care Trust to obtain my records while in care.

By June 2006, I still had not heard anything back, so I filed a complaint with the Consumer Relations Office. I was given the option to contact my previous Social Worker and collect my records, where she would read my notes in her presence and discuss any issues I had. I declined the offer as I was near the end of my pregnancy with our third child, but really, I wanted my notes.

On October 5th 2006, I received a letter from the Chief Executive in relation to the Trust's failure to provide me with a copy of my Social Services records, which I had requested on the 6th February 2006. I received a sincere apology for the unacceptable delay in providing my records. Enclosed in the letter were copies of my records relating to the years 1971 to 1979. They were 'unfortunately' unable to provide later records from 1979 onwards, but would continue to pursue these and the Consumer Relations Officer would contact me if they had any further information.

I wrote to the Trust again in December 2006, to find out if they were able to locate any more of my notes, particularly for the missing years, 1980 to 1994.

On the 6th of January 2007, I received a further letter from the Trust that apologised for the lack of communication. They informed me that the previous letter I received from them, conveyed the impression that I would be updated on the outcome of further searches. This should have occurred and did not. This was due to a misunderstanding on the part of some relevant staff in respect of the communication in the previous letter. The Trust informed me that searches were continuing, but they were having difficulty locating more files due to the many moves that may have affected them over time. They expect re-checks to be concluded by February 2007. I was informed that my previous Social Worker is available to discuss 'any queries you have in relation to my involvement with the Trust, or any records which you have been provided with'. I didn't want to meet her. I just wanted my records.

On the 26th of January 2007, I received further correspondence from the Chief Executive of the Trust to update me on the outcome of their search of my outstanding records. Another apology informing me "that after vigorous efforts they have unfortunately been unable to locate my additional records for this period. The Trust does not believe that any further searches will prove fruitful, such has been the extent of this effort. In the very unlikely event that any further records relating to you are discovered by the trust at any time in the future, I can reassure you that they will be forwarded to you immediately".

Since someone had to be accountable, I wrote to the Information Commissioner's Office explaining my situation. On the 13th of November 2007, I received a letter stating:

"The Commissioner has now received a substantive response from Belfast Health and Social Care Trust about your assessment of processing with our office.

The Trust accepts that they were unable to comply with your initial subject access request within the stipulated 40 day period under the ACT due to difficulties in locating the relevant information. This meant that you did not receive any of the requested information until the 2nd of June 2006 following your initial subject access request in February 2006.

Your second request on the 5th of June for additional information which had not been supplied initially prompted further extensive searches by the Trust for records covering the period approximately 1972-1979. It is my understanding that further information was identified and additional documents forwarded to you on the 5th of October 2006. However the Trust acknowledges that your records from 1979-1993 (they got that year wrong should have been 1994) cannot be traced despite exhaustive searches and for the reasons outlined in my letter to you dated 12th of October 2007.

As well as raising issues of compliance regarding the Seventh Data Protection Principle, the subject access issues in the case also raise concerns about the Trust's compliance with the Sixth Data Protection Principle which states that: - "Personal data shall be processed in accordance with the rights of data subjects under this Act".

On the basis of the information provided to our office, it appears unlikely that Belfast Health and Social Care Trust processed your data in compliance with the relevant provisions of the Act on this occasion.

Unfortunately, it appears there have been breaches of two of the Data Protection Principles in that you were not provided with information within the correct timescale and certain information has been lost. The Trust has been unable to ascertain precisely how long the information from your childcare records has been lost and this matter only came to light when you pointed out that the information provided was incomplete.

South & East Belfast Trust now forms part of the newly established Belfast Health and Social Care Trust as of the 1st of April 2007. The newly formed Trust has assured our office that they will have adequate policies in place to ensure the security of personal data and aim to deal with subject access requests of this nature promptly in the future.

As it appears you have been provided with copies of all the records held by the Trust and they have outlined a satisfactory course of remedial action in light of my assessment. I have no intention of pursuing the case any further. Belfast Health and Social Care Trust has been informed that our office may take this assessment into account if we receive a complaint of a similar nature about the Trust in the future.

Thank you for bringing this matter to our attention."

I was really annoyed with the way the Trust handled my request. If I had not followed up, I would never have heard anything back to this day. I only received scant notes in the end. I felt terribly let down by the State.

In January 2015, I wrote to the Sisters of Nazareth for my records. To enable me to get my records released, I had to provide identification and a signature from a witness to verify it was me. I received one typed page with my name, number, date, when entered, date when I left and baptism date. It was a disturbing response. I felt something was not right, so I contacted them again to obtain further information and asked if they had any photographs while I was living at St Joseph's Baby Home and Nazareth Lodge. They replied in a handwritten letter to inform me that they sadly had no further records belonging to me.

In early 2017, I met a man who was helping survivors and victims of historical abuse. He informed me that my records might be with Family Care Adoption Services, previously known as Family Care Society. I contacted them in early April and on the 27th of April 2017, they presented me with a beautiful, well laid out folder of my records dating from a period between 1977 to 1978. It contained internal case review reports, school reports and summaries of case reviews.

My Life Story Book

ENTERING ADOLESCENCE WHEN my body was physically changing, I found it extremely difficult to navigate my heightened emotions. Inquisitive by nature, I was always passionate to find out about my biological parents and extended family. I always felt I had something missing, leaving an indelible mark on me as a child. I was desperate to find out my identity and who I actually belonged to. At last, after all my questioning, someone was finally listening. In my teens, I was informed that I would be creating a Life Story Book. The concept behind life story work is for social workers to help children in care understand why they don't live with their birth parents. It explains the reasons for entering the care system and events that took place in their early lives. One afternoon in the kitchen, my social worker presented me with a large green photographic book that would eventually contain everything about me.

My social worker did all the research, including photographs she retrieved from both sides of the family. My first task was to delve into my family tree, discovering names of my parents, grandparents, aunts and uncles. But nothing would have prepared me for the complete surprise that I had two half-brothers. I thought there were only three of us. I was curious to find out where they were and why we were separated. I felt the desperate need stirring inside me to meet them. My two half-brothers were sent to another children's home because, as the saying goes, they were from the other side — Protestants. Years later, I was horrified to discover that my granny Campbell was their saviour, rescuing her abandoned Protestant grandsons shortly after they were placed in care.

A note in my care notes:

Mrs. Campbell has guilt feelings about choosing to care for the 'Protestant' children of the family and informed me she would attempt to look after the Flynn children too. Were they

Protestant? *She attributes their falling off in communication to the move to their present area where she says sectarian feelings are high and to the lack of free time now that she has the 2 young children to care for.*

Remember, we were placed in care at the height of 'The Troubles' in Northern Ireland that lasted for about thirty years from the late 1960s to 1998. I was disappointed to read about my granny's decision, however I did fully understand her situation. Religion tears families, communities, and societies apart.

Delving deeper into my family tree felt like assembling the missing pieces of a jigsaw puzzle. My head was spinning wondering, do any of these people know of my existence? Why are these people not looking for me? The stirring up of feelings of rejection and abandonment clung to my soul, which I could not shake off. I was given photographs of family members, who were, inevitably, strangers to me. The social worker gave me information about different family members, and I was instructed to write a few lines under their photograph. I felt the entire process was therapeutic and, at last, I could put names to faces, but the realisation was I had to find these people.

Extract from My Life Story Book

"My name is Isobel Flynn. I was born 30.3.71 in Malone Place Hospital. I weighed xxx. I have no idea what I weighed or what time I was born. I was breastfed for 1 day in the hospital, so I slept in the cot beside my mummy. Other than that I was bottle fed and slept in the nursery. I was woken up at 6.00am and brought up to my mummy to be fed, bathed and dressed. At about 8.00am I went back to the nursery and slept until 11.00am. I then had another bottle was changed and went back to sleep until 2.30pm. There was visiting time at the hospital between 3.00pm—4.00pm at most times my granny Campbell came to visit me. My mummy had her tea after waking and I had another feed, and was changed about 5.45pm. My daddy visited at night between 7.00pm—8.00pm. After this, about 8.15pm my mummy gave me another bottle. I was changed and

went back to the nursery. After 5 days, my daddy came in a taxi and I went home with him and my mummy.

After my shock discovery, I asked my social worker if I could meet my two half-brothers. On the 22nd of August, 1985, I met my two half-brothers for the first time at my foster parent's house. I was excited but nervous. In my angst state, I was desperate to build a bond, just like real siblings. However, to my dismay, although blood related, I had nothing in common with them. They were simply strangers.

Just shortly after my 25th birthday, I felt the urge to find my second oldest half-brother. I remember from our first visit all those years ago that he told me he lived in high-rise flats on a particular road in Belfast. So one Monday morning I was off work and took myself on a mission to find him. The only way I could describe it was like finding a needle in a haystack.

Walking around the area, I asked strangers if they knew where my half-brother lived. After many attempts, someone knew him and pointed me to the high-rise block of flats where he lived. My body was shaking as I was so close to finding him. I cannot remember the exact details of how I knew what buzzer to press, but when I did, a voice came over the intercom and I automatically knew it was him. Within minutes, he arrived at the front entrance and welcomed me with open arms, inviting me up to his flat. I was filled with joy. This time we had so much more in common than during our first visit. We talked for a long time. Things were going really well until his partner unexpectedly arrived. Within seconds I could feel a change of atmosphere and literally before I knew it, he was escorting me out of his flat and accompanying me down in the lift. There he told me he could never see me again. I could not believe what had happened and kept asking him why? He never gave me a proper explanation. My heart was torn and I was in complete bits. I never ever saw him again.

My Mother

AS A PARENT, I've come to truly appreciate the profound role that mothers play in shaping our lives. They are often our first source of comfort, security, and love, influencing not only our childhoods but also the very essence of who we become as adults. For daughters, a mother can act as an anchor, providing a stable presence throughout the journey into womanhood. But when that bond is strained, whether by absence, mental illness, or emotional distance, the effects can be deep and long-lasting. My own experience is a reflection of this reality. A mother's role is deeply personal and multifaceted. For many of us, our mothers become our first role models, guiding us through a world that often demands strength and resilience, especially during times of hardship, like the Troubles. But for others, like me, the absence or emotional distance of a mother leaves a painful void, one that lingers and is nearly impossible to fill, no matter how much time passes. The longing for that genuine connection with your mother, the need for her presence and love, never truly fades.

Extract from My Life Story Book

"My mummy's name was Elizabeth Armstrong. Before she met my daddy, she was married to a man called Ronnie Armstrong. They had two children. My mummy's marriage to Ronnie did not work out so her husband left for Guernsey when young blank was just 18 months old and blank was only three months old. Sometime after Ronnie left for Guernsey, my mummy met my daddy, Brian Flynn. They started going out together and went to live at 3, Bagot Street, Ormeau Road, Belfast. That's the address I came home to when I was brought home from The Mater hospital, Belfast after I was born in 1971."

My mother, Elizabeth Ramsey (née Campbell), was born in Belfast, Northern Ireland, on the *eighteenth of March, nineteen-forty-one*. She was the eldest of six children and the only girl, followed by five boys, including twin boys. She was born in Sandy Row, a working-class area in Belfast. She was a pupil at Linfield Primary School (now a youth club) transitioning to Linfield Secondary School, leaving school aged fourteen, to go to work as a weaver in the Linfield factory in East Belfast. My mother met my father shortly after her marriage ended. I worked that out from the dates of birth of her two sons and my brother being born. I have no idea where or how they met, but they met during the Northern Ireland Troubles, a conflict between Nationalists and Loyalists in Northern Ireland from 1960 until 1998. The conflict was sparked by the demand for civil rights and ended when the Good Friday Agreement of 1998 led to a new power-sharing government, involving representatives from both sides of the community. My mother was a Protestant and my father a Roman Catholic. 'Mixed relationships', or mixed marriages', between Protestants and Roman Catholics during the Troubles were a taboo in Northern Ireland, where church affiliation reflected more than just spiritual belief and was particularly controversial. So, couples often preferred not to publicise their relationships. My father kept his relationship with my mother a secret. Shortly after they formed a relationship, they set up home together in a loyalist area in Belfast where the three of us were born within three years. My mother was very depressed after I was born. On five occasions she stayed away for several days at a time. On Saturday, the 31st of July 1971, aged 4 months, my mother abandoned her children and still hadn't returned by the 3rd of August 1971.

Extract from Care Notes

"Isobel is the youngest of five children born to Mrs. Armstrong. After the birth of her first child Mrs Armstrong had a breakdown and spent several months in Purdysburn Hospital. Her marriage broke up after this and the four youngest children were born out of wedlock. Since Isobel's birth Mrs Armstrong has been very depressed and has left the children with Mr Flynn

(whom she has been living with & who is the father of the three youngest) on five occasions and stayed away for several days at a time. On Saturday 31st July Mrs Armstrong again left the children and hadn't returned home by 3rd August. Mr Flynn then approached us and asked that they be taken into care as he felt he could not cope with their care indefinitely. Mr Flynn himself suffered from depression in the past and it was not considered prudent to encourage him to continue to look after the children.

Since I was a very young child, I always had the desire to see my mother and live with her. Time and time again, I asked people in the children's home and social services if I could see her. That feeling of emptiness of not having a mother present in my life evoked an array of raw emotions and loneliness. I was always told that my mother was unwell and was unable to look after me. But, as an inquisitive child, I often questioned, 'How unwell is she that she cannot look after her own child?' So, after numerous times of questioning, my request was fulfilled.

I had dreamt of this day for so long and no one was going to ruin it. In 1982, aged 11, my social worker brought my mother to my foster parent's house to collect all three of us to visit Belfast Zoo. Peeking out the living room window, I could see a woman, my mother, in the front seat of the car. I could not hold my excitement to meet her and was bursting to get to the car. I had conjured up in my head that my mother would get out of the car, scoop me up and give me the biggest hug ever. But when I got to the car, my mother just sat still in her seat. To my dismay, the social worker told me to get into the car.

After my pleasant but stilted 'hello', my mother appeared to be disconnected and oblivious to what was happening. I tried to strike up a conversation with her but all I was getting was a 'no' or a 'yes', nothing more, she was not reciprocating. Almost in an instant all my excitement of meeting my mother for the first time had been quashed. Thoughts were racing through my head. Why had no one prepared me for this visit? What was wrong with this person? Before I met my mother, I was told she was suffering from post-natal depression, but, of course, that meant nothing to me, nor did I comprehend the severity of her condition. I had no connection with this woman, she was a complete stranger to me. All my dreams of having a loving and nurturing mother were instantly removed from me. I thought, surely, she will get better.

The journey in the car to Belfast Zoo was fraught. There were too many quiet and tense moments where at times you would have heard a pin drop. Rather than my mother caring for my needs that day and asking me everything about myself, the roles were reversed. I was the one checking in with her, asking if she wanted a cup of tea. Her needs were so great that in fact, I felt I was her carer for the day. On my return from the visit, I felt so miserable and incredibly disappointed. All my hopes of having a mother in my life were shattered. I never spoke to anyone at the time about how I felt, nor was I even asked. I really had no desire to see my mother again. What was the point?

As time passed by, I believed in my head that my mother would get better. After persistently asking to see her again, my request was granted. I was desperate to build up a relationship with her and was prepared to give her another chance. In 1983, my mother and my social worker arrived outside my foster mother's house to take us on the ferry to Portaferry and a drive around the Ards Peninsula. Yet again, I found myself in exactly the same situation as twelve months previous. My mother was disengaged and only gave me 'yes' or 'no' answers. My head was screaming inside with frustration and desperation to have a relationship that I imagined with my mother, but no one could ever fix this.

A few years later in 1985, when we moved to the country, another visit was arranged for my mother to visit us at our foster mother's home. By that time, I had come to the realisation that I would never have a genuine reciprocal relationship with my mother. I kind of felt it was my duty to see her. An obligation. That visit was similar to the previous two visits, where she was disconnected and disengaged from everyone around her. I had nothing in common with her but she was my mother and I actually felt incredibly sad to see her the way she was.

In Christmas 1986 our social worker arranged for us to visit our mum, this time in a Psychiatric Hospital in Belfast. I have no memory of who instigated that meeting. I was 15 years old, and had started to comprehend that my mother was suffering from severe mental health problems. She had spent a considerable amount of time at that hospital with various admissions. It was only when I eventually received my care notes many years later that I discovered after the birth of her first child, she had a psychiatric breakdown and spent several months in Purdysburn Hospital.

When we arrived at the hospital we were taken into the visitor's room with tables and chairs. It almost felt like she was in prison, however my mother was not a criminal. She was suffering from chronic mental health problems. My mother was very agitated and withdrawn and could barely string two words together. She was definitely in a worse state than any of my previous visits with her. She was certainly not mentally well enough for visitors, so much so, that I was surprised the hospital had approved our visit that day.

That evening, while travelling home from hospital I mulled a lot of things around in my head. I was gravely shaken by seeing my mother in such an awful state and had made up my mind that it would be the final time I would ever see her.

Just shortly afterwards, I was told that my mother was out of hospital and was much better. I believed she had made a full recovery and was 'normal' again. I was up for another visit. In April 1987 my mother and social worker visited my foster mother's house. Everything that I had fabricated in my head was nothing like the woman I met again. My mother might have been better, but in my eyes, she did not appear to be any different from the times I had met her previously. Even trying to strike up a conversation that we all take for granted with our loved ones, was impossible with her. It was so heart-breaking to say the least. All my hopes of having a mother in my life was never ever going to happen. Accepting that, however, would be another story.

I had no further contact with my mother until 1997, ten years later. I was getting married in Barbados and having a blessing on my return with family and friends. Even though I had never had a relationship with my mother, I felt it was important for her to be there. After all, she was my mother. Before the blessing we all congregated at my foster parent's house for champagne and photographs. The craic was mighty and everyone was enjoying the occasion. In an overcrowded house, my mother arrived, bewildered and disorientated. I was very shocked at how dishevelled she looked, dressed in a pink and grey flowery top, a grey pleated long skirt and ankle boots. I never got that mother's hug, smile or comment on how well I looked, just a stilted 'hello' waiting to be guided by me. This woman had deteriorated even further and it was evident that her mental health had taken hold of her life. Roy had never met her before and whether it was a shock to him, he tried every effort to make her welcome and engage with her.

A year after I got married, I received an unexpected call from my mother to tell me she got married to Hugh Ramsey. I don't even know how she got my house telephone number. I was taken back by her news wondering how a woman with severe mental health could get married. I found it incredibly hard to digest and tried to strike up a conversation with her, but got nothing back. Then, to my disbelief, I could hear a voice, a man's voice in the background, ordering her to hang up and that was the end of our conversation.

My mother rang me sporadically and those calls were very peculiar never striking up a conversation only me asking questions with 'yes' or 'no' answers. When she did ring, I could hear her husband in the background shouting to get off the telephone. It was a sad state of affairs and I was glad when the phone calls stopped.

Around 2008, my brother tried to get in touch with our mum. At that stage, she was back in hospital. The staff informed my brother that my mother had tried to kill herself by setting her nightdress alight with her lighter. She endured horrific burns. Her burns were so severe that it left her disfigured. I was horrified to find this out and it deeply upset me for days, trying to process what happened. I felt helpless because there was nothing I could do.

Just before my 40th birthday, my children had been asking about their biological grandmother. I had told our children about my past when they were younger to make it easier for them to understand why they did not have any biological grandparents on my side. I really had no desires to see her again and felt out of loyalty for my children that it would be best for me to see her first.

In anticipation, I rang Belfast Health and Social Services Trust to check that she was in hospital and arrange a visit. For some unknown reason I gave my mother's married name from her first marriage. I wasn't thinking straight. They took all my details and returned my call several hours later to inform me that she was now living at a Nursing Home beside the hospital where she had been an inpatient for many years. I contacted my Aunt Kathleen, to ask if she was interested in supporting me on the visit. She was delighted to be asked, so off we went on the 11th March 2011 with our bag of goodies and a photograph of my mum and me that was taken at my wedding blessing to give us something to talk about.

Arriving just shortly after 7 pm we met with the matron in charge to check in with her and to take us to see my mum. Suddenly, I decided to show her the photograph of my mum. To my surprise she had informed me, she was not the Elizabeth Armstrong they had living in the nursing home. I was so taken back by her response as the Health Trust had put me through all the security checks needed prior to my visit and there was no way they could be wrong. But they were wrong.

Upset not to see my mother, I suggested to go to the Mater Hospital in the city as I had known she had been in that hospital too. Leaving in a terrible state and wondering where my mother was, I decided to try the psychiatric ward. There, I was met by a male nurse who informed me that he did not know her and to contact medical records the following morning. There was something strange about my conversation with him and the more I probed the more hostile he became. In my heart I felt he was holding something back. It was an awful drive home wondering where my mother could be.

So, the following morning in an anxious state, I contacted Belfast Health and Social Care Trust again. They noted all my details and informed me they would get back to me. I waited anxiously all day then at 7 o'clock in the evening the phone rang. It was the Trust. Again, I was put through the security questions - my name, my sibling's names. To my horror and without any warning, the caller informed me that my mother had passed away. I was in utter shock. My poor mother had died, and no one had ever thought of ever contacting us. I left it too late for me and our children to see her. I asked the caller loads of questions but to my disappointment they could not be answered. I was desperate to find out when she died, how she died and where she was buried.

To my disbelief, the mother who I thought I was visiting turned out to be my sister-in-law who had exactly the same name as my mother before she remarried. She had been married to my oldest half-brother and subsequently died a few years later after my mother.

The reason I know this, is because my half-brother's son contacted me via Facebook to ask if his mother could be buried in the same grave as my biological mother. I explained to him that I did not have the permission to authorise his request as the grave did not belong to me.

The next morning, I rang the Health Trust to find out when my mother had passed away and where she was buried. I was informed the person dealing with my enquiry was on two weeks leave. In my distressed state there was no way I could wait two weeks. So, I begged to speak to the line manager who informed me that my mum had died on the 29th of June 2009, aged sixty-eight. She had been dead for nearly two years and I never knew. Tragically her foot had got caught in her night dress while trying to get out of bed and had fallen onto the floor. It was the impact of her fall, along with her horrific burns from the previous incident that had killed her. Three days after being admitted to hospital, she died. I was so distressed to hear that but, in my heart, I knew she was at peace. I took it upon myself to ring Births, Deaths and Marriage at Belfast City Council who was able to provide me with the grave number and cemetery where she was buried. I was completely inconsolable and cried for hours. Even though I never bonded with my mother, she was still my mother. I was desperate to visit her final resting place and on that same day Roy and I found my mother's final resting place. I was inconsolable, crying for the life we did not have together and how dreadfully sad how it all ended. That was the end of both our journeys.

The head stone inscription read: *In loving memory of a dear husband Hugh Ramsey died 1st October 2005 Aged 60.*

At that stage, there was no inscription on the head stone of my mother. I was shocked to see that Hugh had died so young. I have no idea what happened to him. All I ever knew was that he was blind.

A few weeks later I arranged to see the staff member who had cared for my mum at the hospital. She preferred that I visited rather than chatting on the telephone. Roy and I both went together. I felt perturbed of the visit as I had felt it did not go anywhere. The staff member had nothing to say apart from not being aware that my mum had three other children and that her oldest son and grandson had regularly visited my mum. I was so annoyed with the Health Trust because no-one had cared enough for my mother to check her file that she had other children and to contact us that she had passed away. The Health Trust surely had a duty of care especially to my mother who had been institutionalised in hospital almost her entire adult life. I needed answers. I was not prepared to let this go. The system had failed my mother. Another name and number in a file.

I was adamant to get to the bottom of why we were never told that my mother had passed away. It was eating up inside me so, I decided that it was best to contact my oldest half-brother to ask him why he did not contact us. I had not the faintest idea where my half-brother lived so I decided to write to the Health Trust and ask them to kindly pass my letter on. To my surprise, my brother replied and I contacted him by telephone to meet for coffee in Belfast. I found it incredibly difficult to connect with my half-brother, and decided against asking him why he never tried to contact us. I could see how distressed he was and didn't want to escalate it even further.

Someone had to be accountable for not informing us that our mother had died in hospital. I wasn't going to let it rest so, I wrote to Belfast Health and Social Care Trust and demanded a meeting with their senior staff member. She informed me that my oldest half-brother was my mother's next of kin and it was his responsibility to contact us. I tried to explain to her that we were estranged, as the three of us were put into the care system. She appeared to be completely unperturbed, showing no compassion for my situation. In my raised voice, I told her that the Health Trust had a duty of care for my mother and it was their responsibility to contact us. I let her know that the Health Trust had failed us. I kept reiterating to her the same thing over and over, as she was not just acknowledging or validating how serious my complaint was.

Eventually, she agreed on the failings of the Health Trust. It was huge relief to hear that because it was all I wanted to hear, and that was the truth. Belfast Health and Social Care Trust had failed us; they never gave us the chance to bury our own mother. It would not change my situation but I was determined that no other family had to go through what I went through. She informed me that she would take those lessons back and change things so that no other family would ever have to go through such a horrendous experience. I have often wondered: *Did she just say that to keep me quiet or did she really enforce those changes?*

To my disbelief, a few weeks later, Belfast Health and Social Care Trust rang to ask if I wanted to provide the inscription on my mother's head stone. It came as an enormous shock. Were they carrying some sort of guilt that they felt they had to ask me? I had never done anything like this before but I knew there and then that I was adamant that her five children would be mentioned on the inscription. The Funeral Directors helped me to compose the wording. I found it incredibly difficult making a decision as I had no idea where my other half-brother was living and had been estranged from my 'real' sister.

In the end, I decided to inscribe it with the words:

Precious memories of Elizabeth Ramsey, our mother and grandmother. Died 29th June 2009. Aged 68. From her five children. Called to Rest.

Without warning, Belfast Health and Social Care Trust rang again to ask if I wanted my mother's jewellery as otherwise it would go to the hospital's incinerator. I felt terribly sad about that. It felt to me that my mother was just another patient on a conveyor belt - *when your time's up, let's get rid of your stuff and forget your existence.* I agreed to take it and felt it was something nice to have belonging to my mother. A small envelope arrived with my mum's three beautiful diamond rings and a lighter. When the time was right, a good few years later sitting on my patio in a bright sunny day with my brother and sister I presented them with her rings and let them select one as a keepsake of her.

After my mother died, she left a hand-written note requesting that her savings be left to Belfast Health and Social Care Trust. I did not want any of her money, but I was shocked to hear that she would do any such thing. With all the legalities of a handwritten note it had to go to Probate so the money could be handed over to the Health Trust. After her funeral costs and head-stone inscription, my mother apparently left a large sum of money to the Health Trust. I was disgusted with these people as they had let me down, never making any effort to check my mother's file to see if she had any more children and let me know that my mother had passed away.

My poor mother had an awful life. Mental illness was taboo back in the 1960/70s. If you displayed any signs of poor mental health, mental health services seem to have put that person into psychiatric care, often permanently, instead of being offered counselling, which might have alleviated the problem. Medication was really the dominant treatment. It was the easiest option, but not necessarily the most effective.

People were placed in psychiatric hospitals - in my mother's case, a mental institution - as no-one knew how to properly manage a mental illness. Patients were often sedated, instead of being offered proper therapeutic care. Treatment was inhumane and unorthodox. All too often it was a case of *lock up the person and through away the key*. My mother never stood a chance. As I got older, I came to understand why my mother never made any contact with me. She was unable to. She never functioned at optimal mental capacity. Unable to do anything for herself, let alone find her children. Her absence left a very big void in my life; she was missed terribly as a mother and grandmother.

I was never able to experience the profound emotional bond between a mother and daughter. My desire to have a mother has stayed with me almost my entire life. People often say what you don't have you don't miss. Not in my case as I yearned for a mother's love and to be comforted in her arms. I was never given a mother's love and found it incredibly difficult to show other people love. So, from an early age I would bottle up my emotions to protect me from hurt and rejection. I had always felt a fear of trust and abandonment, and was armoured, wary and defensive. I was too ashamed to tell people why I acted and reacted like I did.

I desperately wanted a mummy who I could share my life with. Someone who would care, support and protect me, laugh and cry with, be there for the good times and bad and do girly things with.

Growing up without a mother left an imprint of psychological scars. The loss, loneliness, grief and sadness were insurmountable at times, where I felt it sucked the life out of me. I carried a lot of pain and felt rejected. I felt robbed, cheated. I resented Mother's Day, a day where others are filled with love, comfort and happiness. It is a day many people take for granted but it was one of those days I dreaded and absolutely hated until I became a mother myself. I struggled at all the different happy milestones such as graduation, getting married, buying our first home together and having our children because my real mother was not there to share my joy and happiness. I knew in my heart I had to accept her absence in order for me to heal and live my life to the best of my ability. The process has been difficult and taken me years to finally accept. And even though I did accept it, it still doesn't stop me from thinking what things could have been like.

Our children were robbed of a grandmother. They had a relationship with Roy's mother, their grandmother who loved them unconditionally and shared all their pivotal milestones. At times it was heart-breaking to watch as I would have loved my mother to be a part of our children's lives. Sadly, it wasn't to be.

Until we meet again, mummy.

Top left: Isabel at Nazareth Lodge, Top right: Primary School
Bottom left: Class Captain Year 8, Bottom right: Confirmation

<table>
<tr><td colspan="3">_Isabel_ El ANNUAL REP... PRIMARY ___1___
Excellent. B   ...d. C = Average. D = Below Average. E = Poor</td></tr>
<tr><td>GLISH</td><td>A</td><td>Oral communication good. Letter formation excellent. Work is neat</td></tr>
<tr><td>THEMATICS</td><td>A</td><td>Has a good understanding of addition and subtraction to 12</td></tr>
<tr><td>ADING</td><td>B</td><td>Isabel is gradually building up the confidence she lacks</td></tr>
<tr><td>REATIVE WORK</td><td>C</td><td>Has produced some imaginative work. Enjoys being creative.</td></tr>
<tr><td colspan="3">RAL REMARKS Mixes well with others, making steady progress</td></tr>
<tr><td colspan="3">ss Teacher D. Flanagan   Principal S Francis</td></tr>
<tr><td colspan="3">MENTS BY PARENT

              Signed ___</td></tr>
</table>

Top left: School report P1, Top right: Isabel's graduation
Bottom left: Isabel in Egypt, Bottom right: Guernsey 1990

Top left and middle: Isabel and Roy's school formal 1987
Top right: Roy, Bottom left: Roy and Isabel

84

Top right: Isabel and Roy, Middle: Aunt Kathleen, Isabel, and Roy
Bottom: Isabel and her mother at her marriage blessing to Roy, November 1997

Nothing Ventured, Nothing Gained

LIFE HAS A WAY of unfolding in the most unexpected ways, especially when we take a chance on an idea that seems far-fetched. The phrase "nothing ventured, nothing gained" is one that has echoed through many pivotal moments in my life. A passing conversation, a spontaneous decision, and the courage to follow through opened doors I could never have imagined. From building a business while raising a family to navigating personal challenges, my journey has been shaped by moments where I simply took a leap of faith. In the pages that follow, you'll get a glimpse into how one small decision can spark a chain of events that reshape your entire world. It's a story about ambition, personal growth, and the balance between chasing dreams and finding stability at home. *My* home. Along the way, there are moments of joy, loss, and everything in between. But more than anything, it's a testament to the rewards that come when we're willing to take risks and push beyond what feels comfortable.

This following is not just about the big wins, it's about the quiet persistence, the unexpected detours, and the resilience needed to turn setbacks into stepping stones. I've learned that sometimes, it's the simplest choices that lead to the most profound outcomes. After all, nothing ventured, nothing gained.

In February 2006, whilst working full time at the arts charity, a fantastic opportunity came my way. The Local Strategic Partnership Board were allocating funding for sustainable projects. After the meeting, as we were going down the stairs, I joked with a girl I knew that we should tender for it as consultants. And to my surprise, she immediately loved the idea. My head went into overdrive and I came up with the idea of working with local community halls, training them on how to manage their hall, secure funding, and how to become sustainable. To my disbelief we successfully secured the tender for two years. Shortly after securing the tender, Roy could see my potential and planted a business idea in my head, which was to set up my own consultancy practice in grant writing and securing funding for registered charities. His idea was more specialised than what I was previously doing and after much deliberation, I decided to set up the business while on maternity leave. Alongside my grant writing, I secured a freelance associate job with an enterprise agency for a couple of years, and before I knew it, I was getting work through word of mouth across Northern Ireland. Anything I didn't know, I just researched, and gradually, over time, I was able to strengthen my skills, knowledge, and experience. Fast forward eighteen years and I still work for myself. It has brought me so much enjoyment and job satisfaction, meeting wonderful people from all walks of life and to this day I still work with some of them.

Then in 2007, we got the best news ever that I was pregnant again. I had always wanted more children. We recently had celebrated our tenth wedding anniversary and had just returned home from Barcelona. Even though things were chaotic at home with the children and work, we were delighted to be expanding our family. Roy and I worked well together, ensuring our family's needs were always met. Despite the chaos of juggling work and parenting, we thrived in it, cherishing every moment. We wanted for nothing, busy juggling the madness of life, we loved it.

Almost nine weeks into the pregnancy, I started to have complications. We took ourselves to the maternity hospital to be scanned. The consultant found the heartbeat and told us everything was fine and the chances of losing the baby were very low. Feeling reassured we took his word. I was scanned again and once again a heartbeat was found beating fast. It was reassuring and we held onto hope that everything was going to work out. Four weeks later, my sickness had gone away and I knew deep down in my heart something was wrong. We took ourselves for another scan to be told our baby had died, our fourth miscarriage. I honestly could not believe this was happening to us again. I found that miscarriage heart-wrenching after being told that there was high chance of our baby surviving. Then came the troublesome question of wanting to take our baby home to bury it. I remember literally just before I was being wheeled into theatre asking the medical team were they sure my baby was dead? I remember reading in a magazine of a celebrity who had miscarried and when she asked them to scan her again the baby was still living. I desperately wanted it to be the same for me. Eleven months later, our fourth baby, our third beautiful son, Calvin, was born. In the end I never got that spring baby that I had planned, it just wasn't to be.

Over the years, my business has brought me great flexibility to raise our family. Even though I was always driven to do well in life, my number one priority was always our children. I wanted our children to have a secure, nurturing and loving environment. In 2014, I decided to give up the child minder and put the children's needs first, working around the business when they were at school. I had the privilege of being off all school holidays. Roy was also entitled to take one day unpaid leave per week until the youngest was 5 and he was an incredible help in looking after the children while I worked one long day per week. I know I put pressure on myself to be a mother and work, but after all these years, I have no regrets. My business enabled us to renovate our home in different stages and most importantly take our children on memorable family holidays abroad nearly every year. The children have been to Spain many times, Italy, Croatia and Lanzarote.

In 2014, I went to Dubai, New Zealand and Australia for a month with Tierna, Ross, and my unrelated Aunt who I love unconditionally. I planned the holiday to precision stopping off at Dubai for three nights, visiting Atlantis Park and seeing the largest building, the Burj Khalifa. There we flew to New Zealand, to the South Island where we hired a camper van and drove to Hanmer Springs and swam in the open hot pools with the snow-capped mountains in the background. We took two exciting boat trips, majestically watching the Giant Sperm whales at Kaikoura and the many pods of dolphins at Akaroa, swimming energetically beside our boat. We visited the zoo and got the chance to feed the giraffes and got into a cage to see the lions up close. After ten days we flew to Sydney and visited the Sydney Opera House, Blue Mountains, Sydney Harbour Bridge and the zoo as well as taking a boat trip to Manley. We then took a flight to Cairns and ventured out to the Great Barrier Reef snorkelling in the open waters to see the beautiful reef and different kinds of coloured fish. Another day we took the train to the picturesque mountain retreat of Kuranda through the world's oldest living rainforest then taking a cable car on our final journey. Returning to Sydney we embarked on a further flight to Perth where I eventually made the trip after all those years of dreaming and stayed with my university friend Manon and her family.

Our biggest family holiday was to Barbados in 2017, celebrating our 20th wedding anniversary and bringing our children back to the place where Roy and I got married in 1997. This had all come about when Roy took out our camcorder on our last day in Barbados asking me "Mrs Kelly, make a wish" I made a wish to return to Barbados on our twentieth wedding anniversary with our children. I was able to fulfil this wish, meticulously saving for ten years.

Shortly afterwards I got the opportunity to travel on two separate holidays to New York and Las Vegas with my foster aunt and foster cousin. We took the most splendid and breath-taking helicopter ride to the Grand Canyon and watching the sun set when we flew back to Las Vegas.

Alongside juggling my own business and our children, I started to help individuals and organisations by fundraising or securing funding for them in a voluntary capacity. I had reached a stage in my life where I was ready and wanted to do something for others. I had never forgotten the struggles that I had encountered growing up and the kindness of people helping me. I was privileged to be in that position, often calling in many favours from my husband, children and friends. Whatever activities the children were involved in, I also secured grants for those organisations on a voluntary basis and became heavily involved with the Parents Teacher Association and the local football club. Over the years, I raised thousands and thousands of pounds, and it was such a feel good factor watching people's faces when I got them money. I was bettering the lives of others.

In December 2023, Tierna and I fulfilled our trip to New York. Having made those plans years before to celebrate a 'big' birthday on the same year, we had to postpone our trip to the Big Apple due to Covid. Opening my New York savings tin, we had enough money to make the trip.

My Father and My Wish to be a 'Daddy's Wee Girl'

FATHERS SHAPE US in ways we don't always realise. For many daughters, their father is the first man they look to for love, support, and guidance, and his presence can provide a sense of stability that carries through to adulthood. But when that relationship is distant, strained, or simply absent, that too leaves a profound sense of loss, one that lingers, no matter how much time passes. My father's absence was a defining part of my life, something that created unanswered questions and a yearning for connection that was never fulfilled. I often wondered what it would have been like to have that bond with him, to feel like 'daddy's little girl,' and to share in those moments that so many others take for granted.

But life had other plans. The reality of my father's struggles, his own demons, and his decision to distance himself from my life left me to navigate that void on my own. The longing to know him, to understand him, stayed with me for years, driving me to search for him, to reach out, and ultimately to face the painful truth that some relationships can't be mended. My experience isn't just about loss, it's about the complexity of seeking something you never had and coming to terms with the reality of that absence. It's about the impact a father's absence can have on a daughter, not just as a child but throughout her life. The journey to find peace with what I missed, and the understanding that some questions may never have answers, is as much a part of my story as the search for my father himself.

My father, Brian Flynn, was born in November 1947 and is the third youngest of eight children. Shortly after meeting my mother, he had three children in quick succession, completing his family when he was barely an adult, himself aged 23.

I often wondered what went through my father's mind when he decided to hand us over to the State. I can only imagine that he must have been in an absolute desperate place mentally and emotionally. Growing up, I often questioned different thoughts in my head. How did he feel about giving up his youngest daughter to strangers? Did he ever think of me? How was he functioning? Did he miss me? Did he ever consider the devastating impact his absence would have on me? And more importantly, why did he never come looking for me? I will never know those answers.

My desire to have a father in my life was not as prevalent as having a mother in my life, though that did not dispel the feelings of still wanting and needing my father. Growing up, I never asked about my father as much as I did for my mother, but I never forgot about him. I do know at one stage he did show an interest in my life when he visited me at the children's home, along with his two sisters, Peggy and Kathleen. I know this, after I received my scant notes when in care. But I have no recollection of any of them visiting me.

The only things I knew about my father when I did my Life Story Book was that he ran a vegetable stall behind Primark in Belfast and had worked in the ship yard. At some stage after it was mentioned he was an alcoholic but it was never recorded in my Life Story Book. I was discouraged by my social worker from meeting my father growing up because of his excessive drinking. In my teens I did not fully understand what an alcoholic was or the implications that surrounded it. However, around that time I started to think a lot more about him and had a desperate yearning to find him.

When I was aged 18, I took matters into my own hands to find my father. Around that time, I had a chance to travel to the Central Library in Belfast with my college class for a research assignment as part of my BTEC National Diploma course. I was never in the city that much so, prior to the visit I hatched a plan in my head to write a letter to my Aunt Peggy and ask her would she tell my father to meet me outside Primark at ten am. I had never had contact with Peggy before then. I found Peggy's address in the telephone book but did not enclose a telephone number.

So, on that day with the camaraderie and craic on the minibus, I was keeping a dark secret from my friends. I did not disclose my plan to anyone. As we reached closer to the city, I began to get more nervous and excited that I was going to meet my father. While everyone was walking to the library, I informed them I had a message to do and would catch up with them later.

In my anxious state I stood outside Primark nervously waiting to meet my father for the first time. I did not know who I was looking for and while I was waiting, I approached two single men who I thought might be my father, but this was not the case. I waited and waited and waited. After ninety minutes, I had to admit defeat. He did not turn up. I was absolutely devastated. I felt so helpless because all my efforts had failed. I could not fully understand why he would not turn up and was tortured about my inner thoughts of him not caring about me. It was the worse feeling in the world. I rarely visited the city and did not know when the next opportunity would be.

My head was all over the place with no one to confide in. My friends knew I was fostered but I was never brave enough to open up or elaborate my situation. I tried to keep my secret from my foster mother as I did not want any ill feelings that I had gone to meet my father and felt she never understood how I felt.

After such a terrible day, Peggy rang my foster parent's house to explain the situation. For some unknown reason, my foster mother took umbrage and hell broke out. I denied everything. My body went into a state of shock and my emotions were all over the place. At that moment I felt I would never meet my father. Thinking that was the end of the saga, I arrived back at college the next day when the principal sent a messenger to my classroom asking for me to see him. I had not the faintest idea why he wanted to see me. He began his conversation by telling me that my Aunt Peggy had rung and just as he mentioned her name my body started to shake uncontrollably. I was aware that I had broken all rules by not attending Central Library and was more worried that I was actually going to be suspended. It took me right back to being in the children's home where I was punished for doing something wrong. In my disbelief he was sympathetic to my situation and actually wished me well in finding my father. I came out of that meeting and cried my heart out.

A few months followed and I asked Roy if he would take me to Belfast to find my father. I decided to visit the market stalls behind Primark as I had retained that information years earlier when doing my Life Story Book. I approached the first person I saw and asked him did he know Brian Flynn? He laughed and said, 'That's Hank'. I explained to him I was Brian's daughter and I was trying to find him. He was amazed my father even had a daughter and shouted all around the other market stalls that I was Hank's daughter. He informed me that my father had not got a fruit stall anymore and told me the bar he drank in and furnished me with his home address.

Almost running to the pub, I was desperate to find him. How would I even know him? What would I say to him? The bar was empty and there was no sight of my father anywhere. I held onto hope as Roy and I still had to go to his house. Finding the house was a big ordeal in itself. There were no Sat Navs in those days. Eventually, we found his house. I could not wait for the engine to be turned off, running like lightning trying to find his house number. I arrived knocking and knocking on the door. But he was not there. I was completely devastated. Did this man want to be found? There was no way I was giving up. I clung onto hope that I would find him. Roy and I returned many times to Belfast over the years, looking and searching. I never did find him.

In the summer of 1994, I decided that I really needed to find my father. I was aged 23 by then and the last five years of my search had been unfruitful. I was living on my own at this stage and it was much easier to keep a secret. The only link I had was my Aunt Peggy. So, I looked her address up again in the telephone book and decided I was going to write a letter to her enclosing my telephone number. I was too afraid to ring her in case she hung up on me. And, hey presto, Peggy rang me. I told her that I would like to visit her with my brother. My plan was slightly devious, as I was really only using her to get to my father. She was delighted to hear from me and we set a date and time to meet at her house. I had involved my brother in the plan too as he also wanted to meet my dad.

Embarking on our journey my brother talked non-stop of his memories as a child visiting Aunt Peggy and Kathleen while he was at the children's home. His memory was that good that he actually took me straight to Peggy's door. Standing at the door was a painfully thin woman who appeared from my first impression to be an alcoholic herself. I didn't find her to be overly welcome considering we were her long-lost family. I found Aunt Peggy to be a strange wee soul and very difficult to hold a conversation with. Really, I had nothing in common with her.

As the afternoon went on, I found she was getting more intoxicated. My brother had mentioned to me in the kitchen that she was filling her cup with vodka as he smelt it off her. The conversation came about my Aunt Kathleen, the oldest member of the family. Whether she was drunk or needed rescuing from us she lifted the telephone up and invited Kathleen over, telling her we were there. After all those years of hearing about Kathleen, I was delighted to have met her in person. She took great delight in her appearance, with pristine blonde hair and elegantly dressed. She had a lovely demeanour and I clicked almost instantly with her. She was ecstatic to see us both, asking mountains of questions about ourselves. She was the first real family member ever to take a genuine interest in me and what I was doing. I asked her about my dad and she told me he was not in a good place and was drinking excessively. I was absolutely devastated. All my hopes of ever meeting my dad suddenly evaporated. Was I ever going to see my dad?

For the next two years, I built up a strong relationship with Kathleen visiting and ringing her regularly. Aunt Peggy was never interested in keeping in touch. Then, in 1996 aged 25, I asked Kathleen if she would help me find my dad. She was very hesitant because of his drinking but in my state of mind I did not completely register how an alcoholic behaved and was adamant to meet him. So, Roy, my brother, Kathleen and I set off on our journey in Belfast to find him. I had not a clue where she was taking us but she appeared to have a reasonable idea where he would be hanging about on the streets. That was a big shock for me because I did not realise how bad his life had spiralled out of control, now living and drinking on the streets. He had a home to live in but had freely chosen to live on the streets. I found it incredibly difficult to comprehend.

Our first stop was at Xtra-vision, a video store at Carlisle Circus in Belfast. My mind was racing and my body was shaking as I was so nervous about meeting him. We followed Kathleen like two lost sheep into the shop, standing behind her. To my surprise, there was my dad propped on the floor looking completely destitute and bewildered. Once he saw us, he got up in a flash. She told him that she had two important people wanting to meet him. The first thing I noticed was his piercing sky-blue eyes. That was one thing I could not deny, I had taken the exact same eyes after him. Behind those eyes he was struggling massively with his own demons. I was so shell-shocked to see him in such a dreadful state and the only way I could describe him was a helpless 'down and out', so drunk and detached from society. When my father looked straight into my eyes, he knew exactly who I was with tears running down his face.

He was so drunk that he couldn't even string a few words together. My brother tried to strike up a conversation with him while I stood completely frozen and oblivious to the situation. My father that I had longed to meet all those years was just like a stranger to me and the disappointment was gut-wrenching. I returned back to the car in floods of tears, more so because I knew in my heart that I would never able to build a relationship with him unless he miraculously gave up the drink. I was so relieved that Roy never got the chance to meet him only because I was too embarrassed and ashamed.

A few weeks later, we arranged to meet my father again, this time at Kathleen's house. She had been in touch with him to let him know about the arrangements. I was hopeful for this visit as I thought he would have got his act together and tried. However, my father had other plans going on and never turned up. Kathleen had an idea where he might be and asked Roy to drive her to him. Around fifteen minutes later they all arrived back with my dad in tow. To my horror, I was met by a drunk man who did not know where he was, talking a load of gibberish. He looked hideous, unkempt and unshaven in a long coat, holes in his shoes, and a can of lager hanging out of his pocket and nicotine fingers.

My father had become dependent on alcohol as a coping mechanism to eradicate his pain[2]. I believe my father turned to drink to relieve his suffering after losing his children. I cannot imagine how he must have felt all those years. It appeared to me that he simply just gave up on life.

Through conversations I had with Aunt Kathleen, she told me that my father was a successful businessman, running his own fruit shop. Even though I knew very little about him, my father was a grafter. I had definitely inherited his traits when it comes to working. I started working part time from the age of thirteen, and have continued to work, often juggling two or three jobs at the same time. Just like my father, I have always been business minded and for the last eighteen years I have been running my own grant writing business and more recently mentoring and working with our son Ross in his coffee business. I find that comforting. It is just a pity that we never got to share our similarities and business ideas together.

Another five years drifted by without seeing him when Kathleen contacted me to let me know that my father had been admitted to a nursing home. It really only evolved because he had gone into hospital to get an operation to reset his arm that he had broken six months previously and had done nothing about. He was in complete agony and needed to get it attended to immediately. While in hospital the medical team had advised Kathleen that he should go into a nursing home because he had early stages of Alzheimer's brought on by his excessive drinking. He was still living on the streets then.

---

[2] At that very moment I realised that alcoholism had taken a deep place in his soul. Alcoholism, referred to as alcohol use disorder, occurs when someone drinks so much that their body eventually becomes dependent on or addicted to alcohol. Alcohol use causes complex changes to brain chemistry which are believed to contribute to the development of alcoholism. (source www.healthcare.com).

It was only out of a sense of duty that I went to visit him at the nursing home as I thought that because he had stopped drinking, I would to be able to have some sort of conversation with him. But sadly, my expectations were again dashed from the very moment I walked into the room. My father talked no sense whatsoever. I felt no connection or feelings towards him. I was devastated. All my hopes of ever even having a conversation and building a relationship with this man were instantly perished. There was simply no point. Why would I torture myself again? But I did torture myself and out of guilt I returned to see him again at the nursing home a few months later, this time with Roy. It was really a disappointing visit and I decided that it was going to be my final visit.

A decade passed and I still stuck to my word, I never returned back to visit my dad. At times, I did think about him. I was too busy looking after our own children by then and working. From time-to-time Kathleen mentioned him in conversation but nothing had changed. I had no desire to visit him again.

When I was in my early forties, Roy had suggested for me to take our children to meet my father. Initially, I was taken aback but guilt had set in because he was, after all, the children's grandfather. In 2016, I brought Tierna, Ross and Craig to meet him along with my brother. Calvin, our youngest son, was too young to meet him and would not fully understand. I had prepared the children for what he might be like and explained that he had early stages of Alzheimer's. My dad had moved into another nursing home and appeared to be settled. When we arrived, my father recognised my brother instantly. He wasn't making any sense, and there was no way we were going to get any coherent conversation out of him. The children appeared to be laughing at him, not with him. It was so disappointing for the children to witness. That afternoon when travelling back in the car I had made my mind up that it was going to be my final visit with him.

Then something unreal happened. In March 2017 at a local restaurant with some friends after tragically burying their brother, I got speaking to a friend of their family. She went on to tell me she was originally from Belfast. I was very surprised with this, telling her I was, too. For some unknown reason I asked her did she by any chance know a man called, Brian Flynn. And, to my surprise, she knew my father! I told her that I was his daughter and she was flabbergasted. She called her brother over to tell him what she discovered, and suddenly he broke down in tears. To my disbelief, it turned out that he was my dad's best friend at school. When he told my friend's mum who I had known from a teenager, she just could not believe it, as it turned out that she had met both my Aunts, Kathleen and Peggy, several times as a teenager herself.

To my surprise, in October 2019, our youngest son Calvin aged 9, asked Roy could he meet his grandfather. Calvin never instigates things so, I felt it was important to visit him again. In November 2019, Calvin and Craig along with my brother and his girlfriend went to visit my father in the nursing home. When we arrived, my father recognised my brother instantly. My father thought I was his oldest daughter and called me by her name. Calvin was wearing his Manchester United football strip, which sparked my father to reminisce about football. Calvin really engaged with him and although my dad talked nonsense, Calvin had a great laugh with him. I held no conversation with him although one thing that was striking on the day was when my dad said, 'As long as you are happy.' My initial thoughts were that this man, my father, still knows nothing about me. But perhaps he could clearly saw that I was happy and maybe he was relating to that, who knows?

In March 2020 the coronavirus pandemic arrived and the whole country was on lock down. At the end of that April, I got a message from my cousin to ask me to urgently ring her mother, my Aunt Kathleen. When I phoned her late in the evening, I was told that my father had Covid-19, and was in hospital for a week, gravely ill and was unlikely to pull through. A deep feeling of sadness came over me. What an awful way to die. I got onto the prayer team immediately and prayed myself. I was deeply upset. And even though I had struggled to have a relationship with my father over all those years I was very sad to hear that he was going to die, all alone.

For the next few days, we got a daily update from my Aunt Kathleen. His temperature was sky high and they were unable to put him on a ventilator because he was over seventy and had underlying health issues. By the tenth day my dad's temperature started to go down and within forty-eight hours he had been discharged from hospital. This man had miraculously recovered and was a born survivor like his own daughter.

My father is still living in a nursing home. He has been diagnosed with Wernicke-Korsakoff syndrome, alcohol-related dementia, which is a type of alcohol-related brain damage. His days of drinking alcohol have caught up with him and have taken hold of his life. He struggles with day-to-day tasks and cannot do anything for himself such as have a conversation or make any decisions, but is able to walk unaided. I have no plans to visit him again and I am at peace with that. One day I know I will get that telephone call to tell me that my father has passed away and I know it will be a painful and sad time, grieving for the life that I could have had with my father that never happened.

Growing up without a father in my life has been one of the most painful and traumatic experiences. My emotional deprivation from an absent father has without a doubt left an indelible emotional scar due to the deep sense of loss and overwhelming sense of abandonment. I missed the absence of a healthy relationship with my father, with the child within the adult longing for love and connection, craving what I never ever got to experience. I never got the opportunity to be daddy's wee girl. His absence led me to a sense of unworthiness and identity issues. It affected various aspects of my life as he was not there to watch me grow up, graduate, get married and become a mother to his grandchildren. Despite the pain I encountered without my father, confronting my feelings through counselling provided me with a space to understand the consequences, navigate my emotions and adopt effective coping strategies to overcome my challenges to enable me to lead a fulfilling life.

Our four children missed out terribly from not having a grandfather present in their lives. Roy's father had died before any of the children were born. I have noticed over the years how his absence from their lives affected them. They, too, suffered loss and pain, unable to build a relationship with him and to share exciting and memorable moments at different times in their lives. I feel it the most when they talk about their friends and the relationships they have with their grandfather. Sadly, I cannot change the situation but it does bring me great pain of what could have been for them in their lives if they had a grandfather.

Gillian, Alison and Me

BELONGING IS SOMETHING we all crave—a sense of being rooted, connected, and understood. For some, it comes naturally through family, friends, or community. But for others, like me, the journey to find that sense of belonging is winding and unpredictable. It's not always about where we come from, but about the people we meet along the way who help us feel truly seen and valued. It's about those unexpected connections, those individuals who come into your life at just the right moment and fill gaps you never knew were there. These later-in-life relationships brought me a sense of home and identity I had long been searching for.

My path to belonging wasn't straightforward and often left me questioning where I fit in. The search goes beyond family ties; it's about finding your place in the world and understanding where you come from, even when the way forward feels uncertain. What I share in the following pages reflects on those pivotal moments of connection—moments that brought clarity and peace after years of searching. This is a story of how relationships can transform, heal, and provide the belonging we all need.

I found a 'real' cousin on my mother's side in 2011. It was a breakthrough for me as I had no contact on that side of the family. I found Gillian just by chance when I found my oldest half-brother, after finding out the shock discovery of my mother's death. He had mentioned Gillian in a conversation. I then went looking for her on Facebook. Gillian and I met in a restaurant just before my 40th birthday in March 2011. We formed a bond almost immediately and had so much in common. I had brought my Life Story Book with me which had my family tree. It was so nice going through it and finding out about the rest of my family. To this day, we keep in touch and see one another regularly. She is like a sister to me and I love her unconditionally. After I found Gillian, I decided that was the end of my journey of searching for my real family. I had found what I needed and more.

Embroiled in a busy life, I was still in contact with my Aunt Kathleen who I had first met way back in 1996. By that time, I had met her family and was invited to her daughter's wedding in 2014. Unbeknown to me I was introduced to another cousin, Alison, who had lived in England all her life. Her mum and my dad were siblings. I found out about Alison when I was doing my Life Story Book but it never crossed my mind to contact her. Alison and I instantly clicked and to this day she is a big part of my life and I love her to bits. I call her my 'real' cousin because even though I had cousins growing up in foster care they were weren't really my 'real' cousins. We have a right wee laugh about that now and even when I introduce her to people, I always emphasise the word 'real'. I suppose, for me, it really is a sense of belonging to a 'real' family.

In July 2022, Tierna graduated from Queen's University of Belfast. It was one of the proudest moments of my life. She works in politics and is a councillor for the Alliance Party in Northern Ireland. She was the first and youngest woman to be elected within the Rowallane area. On the 6th of April 2024, Tierna and Noah got married. It was such an emotional day seeing her walk down the aisle with her dad and speak publicly of her idyllic childhood. Her wedding day was so amazing and to see them both so happy brought joy to my soul.

I am extremely proud of all our children despite them thinking I have a favourite! I do keep them going, sure isn't that what mothers do? I know I was the protective mother and at times I moved mountains to make sure that I could provide for them and give them the unconditional love and support they deserve. I was there for every milestone they reached.

When the children were born, I set up a memory box for each of them which eventually I had to move into larger storage containers because I had accumulated so much stuff. I kept everything for them – cards, first tooth, first strand of hair, first shoes, drawings, photographs from school, everything you could possibly think of. When they eventually leave home, they will get their memory box to take with them. I recently gave

Tierna her memory box and when we started to go through it, we were both amazed at how much stuff there was, jogging our memories and bringing back incredible times. I had nothing given to me from my childhood and I knew how life changing this would be for the children to have something that belonged to them.

I never wanted my children to experience the poverty that I did when I left care, so when they were born, I opened a trust fund for them putting every penny I had and money given to me by family and friends so they could access it when they were 18. I wanted them to have a better start than I ever did.

I struggled terribly when they all reached the age of 4 months and 7 years. Those milestones were more poignant to my life when I was handed over to the State and left the children's home. With the child in me, I compared their lives at that stage to the life I had, which brought me considerable sadness as to how my life could have been. When our children were growing up, I found it incredibly difficult to control my emotions, such as attending the doctor, hospital, school plays, or parent meetings. Tears would drip down my face, but they were tears of distress and mostly of joy. Their pain was my pain, their joy was my joy. Roy often tells me I spoilt our children. I never saw that as I wanted them to have a better childhood than I had. I consciously made sure that I didn't off load my trauma onto them. I feel I have brought them up to be well grounded, independent, kind and thoughtful children. It brings me great delight when they tell me they had such an amazing childhood. Calvin, recently told me that Roy and I are his inspiration. Really, we couldn't ask for anything more.

We were both fortunate to have had the support from Roy's mum and sister with the children. Roy's sister is seventeen years older than me, and became my surrogate mother, willingly helping me when she could and played a massive part in our children's lives. Sadly, Roy's mum passed away and his sister has Alzheimer's, a cruel disease.

Returning to the Theme of Trauma

TRAUMA HAS A way of shaping us long after the events that caused it. It seeps into the everyday, influencing our thoughts, our behaviours, and the way we cope with the world around us. For me, the realisation that I was living with unresolved trauma didn't come overnight. It was a slow awakening, one that took years to fully understand. Over the years, I have reflected a lot on the difficult journey of confronting my past. In my early twenties, I thought I had control over my life, but deep down, I was using all the wrong methods to mask the pain. It wasn't until someone close to me pointed out the dangerous path I was on that I realised I needed to make a change. That moment sparked a shift in how I viewed my trauma and my own responsibility in healing from it. The stigma surrounding mental health back then made it hard to admit that I needed help. I feared being judged, misunderstood, or worse, ignored. But eventually, I found ways to confront my struggles, slowly working on changing my mindset and unlearning the negative patterns that had taken root. Through counselling and sheer determination, I started to rebuild myself, finding healthier ways to cope with the lingering pain. Along the way, I discovered the importance of connection, learning how to open up, accept love, and give it in return. But this did not come without 'setbacks'.

When I eventually made it to university, I enjoyed the freedom of being on my own. I was drinking excessively to get through my pain as I still did not know how to manage it. A telephone conversation that I had with Roy when I was 20 years-old was the first wake-up call. He told me that if I continued to keep drinking the way I was I would turn out like my father. That scared the living daylights out of me and made me realise that drink was never the answer. Nowadays, I rarely drink and I believe his words saved me.

Around the age of 21 I realised I was dealing with trauma. The trauma I experienced wasn't the event or experience itself, but my body and mind responding to it. In my conscious mind, I realised that the only person who was going to fix me, was myself. Struggling with mental health problems in the 90s was a taboo subject with stigma and judgement attached to it. I was never brave enough to go to the doctor to discuss my struggles as I was too afraid that he would think I was not coping and prescribe me with medication. No magic pill was going to get rid of my pain. My negative thinking patterns were creating unnecessary stress and anxiety and if I did not do something about it, I was paving the way for a bleak outlook in my life. I started to slowly work on my inner self, changing my mindset by accepting what happened to me could not be undone. With hard work over a long period of time I gradually retrained my brain, replacing negative thought patterns to positive thoughts.

I realised that not only was I dragging myself down but I was dragging other people down with me. I kept myself distracted, mainly by working as it was my coping mechanism as well as reading, walking, writing, listening to music or whatever to improve my life. I was so used to people putting me down all the time as a child, I struggled to accept praise when it was being offered. I still have difficulties with that today, palming it off and changing the subject, but I am getting better at managing it.

I changed my mindset from feeling like a failure to someone who would succeed. I started to believe in myself, always repeating and telling myself that I am brilliant and can do anything. I still do that today. I taught myself how to love myself and to show love and affection to others.

I found it incredibly difficult to show love and affection because I was never given it. I remember the first time when a friend hugged me and I was like a brick. I had never been hugged before and reciprocating that was really difficult for me. So, in order to do this, I deliberately observed people's behaviour at train stations, bus stations, airports or wherever. This taught me how to be more socially responsive with my emotions and after reinforcing it time and time again helped me to naturally hug and show love to people. I surrounded myself with positive people and have been fortunate to find incredible friends who have influenced, encouraged and inspired me on my journey and are still there in my times of need.

I started my journey with counselling when I was 23. I was struggling with trauma and needed external help. Despite my financial woes, I was determined to feel better in myself. Counselling allowed me to process my emotions and feelings and learn new strategies to deal with my trauma. I returned to counselling on and off for almost three decades until I met a pastor from a new church I joined. He told me I needed to forgive the people who had caused me so much harm. I thought why would I do that?

Aged 28 I started to talk about writing my book and by the age of 31, I started to write my book. I was really in a good head space and had made substantial progress with dealing with my trauma. I was living life to the full and had everything I had dreamed of, and more. I was very happy and satisfied with my life. I felt I needed to share my memoir with others so people could understand the harsh reality of growing up without biological parents and the difficulties and obstacles navigating through Northern Ireland's care system, inspiring others to never give up on hope. I contacted a professor at Queen's University of Belfast who was interested in helping me. I met him a few times then contact ceased as I was too busy looking after our children and setting up my business. Periodically, I returned to writing the book. Then in 2018, a very good friend of mine offered to help me write my book and that continued for another three years on and off. But my ambition to write my book never left me. In 2019, I was at a Prophetic night and someone randomly came over and spoke a word to me, telling me that my past was my biggest weapon and to use it. Here I am twenty-five years later and have achieved my dream to become an author. Writing this book has been the hardest and best thing I have ever done. At times it was incredibly painful, but after taking some time out I felt the urge and determination to keep writing. I wanted and needed to share my story.

In September 2021 I approached Wave Trauma Centre. I had been researching for someone to help me through my recent trauma (that will come later) and came across their website. I discovered they were providing support to survivors and victims of Historical Institutional Abuse and the timing really came at a crucial time in my life. I was eligible to receive support and help for my physical health and emotional wellbeing that was funded by Victims and Survivors (VSS). The charity offered me a counsellor who still works with me. Her invaluable support and knowledge have helped me to channel my emotions and find strategies and tools to navigate through my recent upheaval. I have been offered a long range of support towards helping me with my physical health and was sent privately to investigate the struggles I was encountering with my feet. I have never been on benefits in my life and getting that kind of support has been phenomenal to receive. The different feet specialists never got to the root of my problem. However, more recently I spoke to my brother-in-law who is a doctor and he informed me that my feet were sore because of the stress I was under. That made sense to me as I had been carrying a heavy burden for so long.

In May 2023, my case worker offered me the opportunity to attend a Trauma and Body four-week course run by Wave Trauma Centre. It was not trauma therapy but information on what trauma is and how to regulate the body. I never had that sort of information on hand before and receiving it has been so invaluable helping me to manage my thoughts and regulate my body much better when it becomes unregulated.

Having a positive attitude has helped me massively throughout my life. I tend to focus on the positives of my life and even when things get difficult, I try to take something good from that. However, nothing would have ever prepared me for what was to come next for me and our family.

An Incident at Home and the Awful Aftermath

THIS CHAPTER DELVES into an experience that no family expects to face, a moment that reshaped everything we thought we knew about stability and security. What unfolded was something beyond our control, leaving us to navigate a difficult path that tested the very core of who we are. It's was a time filled with uncertainty, where the ripple effects of one incident impacted every aspect of our lives. The weight of responsibility became overwhelming, as we tried to piece together solutions in a situation that felt impossible to fix. The emotional toll of watching a loved one, especially a child, suffer in ways we couldn't have foreseen was unbearable. Alongside this, financial pressures mounted, adding yet another layer of difficulty. The fear of losing everything we had worked so hard for became a constant shadow, amplifying the strain already weighing us down.

I don't just focus on the struggle itself but on how such unexpected hardship can alter the dynamics of a family. It's about how we cope, the lengths we go to protect those we love, and the immense pressure that comes with trying to hold everything together when the world feels like it's falling apart. At its heart, this whole experience was, and is, about resilience. It is about the quiet strength that emerges in the face of adversity, and the glimmers of hope that keep you pushing forward, even when the road ahead seems unclear. There are no easy answers, but through it all, we learn that sometimes the only way out is through, step by step, even when you don't know what's waiting on the other side.

It brings me immense sadness and pain to write this chapter. I would have never thought in a million years that this would have ever happened to us as a family. Tragically, a few years ago there was an incident at our family home with other people. We are so remorseful for what happened. Due to legal reasons, I am unable to tell you in detail of the events which unfolded. I do apologise for this and I hope you can understand my decision. Nothing would have ever prepared us for what yet was to come.

Soon after this incident, our youngest son, Calvin, gradually stopped eating. Then, we received correspondence from a solicitor which confirmed compensation was being claimed following the incident. My heart sank, as I had let the house insurance lapse, an oversight on my behalf. We had assets, our home and if we could not pay up, our house would have to be sold. We had paid off the mortgage much earlier than planned and everything we worked so hard for all our married life was at risk of being lost. Completely.

Our dreams and our plans for retiring early were suddenly taken away from our reach. Everything was falling apart. I had to get a plan in place, quickly, before we all fell apart.

Almost overnight without any warning my body went into menopause. While my body battled to adjust with night sweats, day sweats, tiredness, and short term memory loss, I simply didn't have time to manage my symptoms or feel sorry for myself. I had other bigger priorities to deal with.

Calvin was deteriorating in front of our very eyes. Although not yet diagnosed, we knew he was battling with an eating disorder. His weight had plummeted and he had extreme anxiety. In order for any of us to survive on a daily basis our brain needs 500 calories alone. Calvin was not even consuming that amount which often left him delirious and weak. He was also exercising excessively pacing the living room for hours and secretly doing weights.

I had taken him to the GP who referred him to CAMHS (Children and Adults Mental Health Services), which specialised in eating disorders. They had an 18-month waiting list. Calvin could not wait that long, as both his mental and physical health were deteriorating rapidly. I spent every waking hour researching the internet, desperately trying to get him private help. But thrust upon me was long waiting lists.

I had managed to find him a counsellor in the interim period, but even she struggled as she had not got the experience to deal with his eating disorder.

Fifteen long difficult and stressful months had passed since the incident and we decided to take Calvin away for a few days to Portrush to try and lift his mood. He refused to eat and his anxiety was at an all-time high. I was so worried about him. When we returned from our short break, I immediately took him to the Royal Victoria Hospital. He desperately needed intervention. The professionals did not appear to be too worried about him and because he was not suicidal, they were unable to admit him. But Calvin did have suicidal thoughts, they were just not listening enough and did not care. But I cared.

A few days after our disappointing trip to the hospital, Calvin hit me hard. This was not in Calvin's nature and I knew in my heart that his eating disorder was starting to ravage his body and take over his mind. He was delirious and not making any sense. I had been baking that day for Ross and his coffee business as we had a busy bank holiday weekend ahead. As his mother, I knew something drastic was wrong so I immediately contacted the eating disorder team, crying down the telephone in a frantic state that he was very ill. There I was instructed to take him straight to the Ulster Hospital, where a bed would be waiting. At last, someone was listening and taking me seriously. After we attended triage, he was immediately taken to the children's ward. My gut instinct was right, he was deteriorating rapidly and needed medical help immediately. Calvin's heart beat was extremely low and he was gravely ill. The hospital's priority was to get him medically well and were not concerned with his mental health. However, I learned fast that the two go hand in hand but no one was joining the dots.

Calvin was not allowed any exercise in hospital and even to go to the toilet he required a wheelchair. I was allowed to take him outside around the hospital grounds, but only in the wheelchair. Although, I cheekily broke those rules. I took him further, to the park, Asda, Stormont and to meet family and friends at McDonald's. He was in hospital during Covid and was not allowed visitors so they met him outside of the grounds of the hospital. As his mother, I tried everything to raise his spirits. His sister, Tierna, visited him regularly. She was struggling with his illness as well as the civil case hanging over our heads. Every day, I took him to the hospital chapel to pray. I prayed out loud with him and he would listen. Praying to God was my only sanctuary. I was desperate for a miracle to get him well again. I found it extremely difficult to cope with my emotions. I was engulfed in my own pain and cried at the slightest thing, especially when the nurses and consultants spoke with me. They had no idea the burden I was carrying. I begged God to give me the strength to get through this nightmare.

In the midst of my mayhem, I had an inclination that Calvin was autistic. He had been assessed when he was three years of age, because he had all the classic symptoms of not meeting milestones, poor behaviour, slow walker and a speech impediment. But the consultant, had made the decision that he was not autistic. However, he continued to have struggles through primary school and deep in my heart I knew he was. When he was admitted to hospital, I asked for him to be assessed. At that time, we were told there was a long waiting list. He could not wait that long. I spent hours researching for a private autism assessment and eventually found one. They had a waiting list of six months. I checked with them to see if their assessment was recognised by the Health Trust and Education Board, as I did not want to put him through all of the upheaval to be told that it would not be recognised. The company I selected had a track record of assessments accepted by both statutory agencies, the Health Trust and the Education Authority. Calvin was privately assessed and it was confirmed he was autistic. The diagnosis was life changing for Calvin as he could now be himself without having to mask his autism at home. He did tell me that he still can't be himself in public and at school and tries to act 'normal' because if he didn't, he would be disruptive, loud and annoying to teachers. His courage to speak up and share with others tells you what struggles an autistic child has to cope with daily.

I found it incredibly difficult to process how the hospital dealt with a patient with an eating disorder. They followed a strict eating plan within a set time to eat. If the patient does not eat their food, they are forced to drink a high calorie shake. I challenged them many times, as my research was telling me you are not allowed to force a person with an eating disorder to eat, but they kept telling me that were there to keep Calvin medically safe. I found the whole process very frustrating. Calvin broke every rule to avoid eating so, inevitably, they had to resort to inserting a feeding tube down his throat. For the first few days, he seemed attentive. Then, he complained that it was hurting his throat and pulled out the feeding tube. I know the medical team were doing their job, but some of them lacked compassion and experience to deal with an autistic child, which I found distressing to watch. He was also highly medicated to suppress his mood and get him to sleep. Even getting him to take this medication was a nightmare and he refused any medication that was in tablet form.

After two weeks in hospital, I was told that I had to see the dietitian at the eating disorder unit across the city. She had informed me that I must treat Calvin's eating disorder as if he had cancer. Even that word frightened me, as in my head I thought he was going to die. I was so vulnerable and desperate to get him help, that everything they said I took quite literally. It was a daunting journey and at times I felt so alone as I wasn't educated enough about an eating disorder, and had no idea how to help Calvin navigate it. A week later, Calvin and I met with the mental health nurse at the eating disorder team. That in itself was such a big ordeal, getting him from the hospital to their place, as he had to be taken in a wheelchair to the car. Trying to get parked outside a busy hospital in a wheelchair with a sick child caused me so much anxiety. At our first visit it was confirmed that Calvin had Disordered Eating. No one ever explained to me what that was. To my disbelief all they talked about was food and that raised his anxiety levels even higher.

After six weeks, Calvin was discharged from hospital even though he had lost nine pounds that week. It was as if they were giving up on him. Ten days later, Calvin became delirious again and was not talking any sense. When I rang the eating disorder team in a distressed state, they advised me to take him to the hospital. This time there was no bed waiting for him. Eighteen long hours later in the middle of the night Calvin was admitted back into the children's ward. A team of medical staff had been waiting for him. My gut instinct had been right again, Calvin was gravely ill and his heart beat was low. It was as if he had just given up on life and wanted to die. It was so painful to watch. The medical team along with Roy had to restrain him to insert a feeding tube to get enough food into him before he pulled the feeding tube out. His life was hanging in the balance. I was in absolute bits and one of the nurses took me away as she saw how distressed I was. The next few days were critical and eventually they were able to stablise his heart rate. We were all exhausted, especially me, as I was spending every minute I had with him at the hospital.

While in hospital, his 13th birthday was looming in the background. He was not well enough to be discharged so I asked if it was possible to take him home for a few hours. The medical team agreed only on the condition that he ate something. Roy and I arrived at the hospital at 10 am excited to take him home. We had taken his dog Duke to cheer him up. When we arrived at the hospital his anxiety was at an all-time high, with the nurses and doctors reiterating to him that he would only get home if he ate something. I think if they had backed off, he would have eaten in his own time. You are probably thinking sure if you coaxed or bribed him surely he would eat. Yes, you would have thought that. But it does not work like that with someone who has an eating disorder. The mind is complex. Desperate to get him to eat we asked to take him to the hospital restaurant. It was on their terms, as long as we took photographic evidence of him eating.

After two grueling hours in the restaurant eventually he ate some food. Eight hours later, we eventually left the hospital with the conditions we had to have him returned within four hours. We were conscious we had a two hour round trip and every minute was precious with him. His siblings had all being waiting patiently for him at home. It was so lovely to have him home for his birthday, though we were all tenterhooks as he was struggling with his anxiety. I found it very distressing bringing him back to hospital. I was in floods of tears because he really needed the mental health intervention now, to help him, but the medical team had other priorities.

After four weeks in hospital Calvin was discharged. I was determined to keep him out of hospital this time. The only way I was ever going to do that was to educate myself about eating disorders and to find him the private help which he needed, and so deserved. My business had to go on hold for the foreseeable future, as I was his main carer. After spending numerous hours researching, I came across a charity called BEAT Eating Disorders. They were incredibly helpful and I attended online training via Zoom. Listening to other people's stories was disturbing and unsettling, but I was not alone in this journey. Shortly afterwards BEAT sent me an email offering me to apply for a one-to-one coaching support programme for carers supporting a loved one with an eating disorder. A twelve-week programme delivered by an experienced BEAT advisor. I was relieved when I got accepted. They provided me with a carer's eating disorder book and every week waiting patiently on my forty-minute telephone call I was able to gain a stronger insight into Calvin's eating disorder, learn some practical techniques and help to motivate positive changes in his life.

I was educating myself about an eating disorder and was able to apply this to Calvin. I learned fast that it was important to build Calvin's confidence and tell him how brilliant he was and that I loved him. Even though he never reciprocated, those are the building blocks for any person with an eating disorder. The biggest thing that stood out for me - and I am still conscience today - with any young person or any person is to never tell them how well they look and have put weight on. We as humans sub-consciously internalise everything and may be the trigger that starts or restarts an eating disorder. I was advised to focus on a piece of clothing, shoes or jewellery, letting them know you love it or whatever. When back at home, Calvin refused all medication, so I made the decision to monitor his mental health on a daily basis. I got him involved in scoring how he was feeling every day out of ten and if it reached below three, I knew I was in trouble. Miraculously, it never went below.

I eventually found him another private therapist, paying extortionate money and driving for hours, which left him agitated. My gut instinct was telling me it was not the right help for him so I found someone else. I hated making these changes, but as his mother I knew it was the right decision. In my heart I felt nothing was working. He was not eating and his mental health was deteriorating even further.

Our visits to CAMHS were abysmal and non-consistent, cancelling appointments and constantly changing his support worker. They were more interested in getting him to eat and talking about food, as opposed to treating the mental health side of an eating disorder. It was the continuity of care that he needed and someone who was able to work on the mental health side. I had an awful feeling that the staff were not experienced and knowledgeable enough to treat a child with an eating disorder.

The psychiatrist recommended Calvin a new medication. But when I did the research, it was to treat schizophrenia. I challenged why and got shot down immediately and was simply told to make a decision. As far as I could see, pumping medication into Calvin was not the solution to deal with his mental health. I had become less vulnerable and had started to challenge the professionals. I was so disappointed with the level of care Calvin was being offered.

Calvin was unable to return back to school and start Year 9. I contacted the school to get some work so I could do it with him in the hospital and at home. I only managed thirty minutes of school work per day because his level of concentration was poor due to not eating. I was conscience of him missing so much school. It was only through a conversation with someone I knew that I found out he was eligible to be home schooled. Three months after I applied, Calvin was home schooled by the best teacher ever. That was one thing about Calvin; he always liked school and engaged well with his teacher. I cannot thank her enough for what she did for Calvin.

Eventually, I found him a play therapist. She was amazing with him and I started to see small green shoots of progress.

His mental health was improving, and he was positively talking about his future. That in itself was a breakthrough.

My next big challenge was to get him back to school. However, in order to get him the help he needed, I had to apply for what is called a Statutory Assessment to the Education Authority. The mountain of paperwork was unreal but with my great organisation skills I was able to get through it. The School Psychologist, was one of the nicest people I ever met. After her assessment she recommended that Calvin got a full-time classroom assistant. I jumped for joy as I was so relieved that he was finally getting the help and support he needed.

His private autism assessment had to be ratified by the Health Trust. I was shocked to see the consultant who had assessed him all those years ago had approved this. I wondered if she ever remembered him.

After one academic school year of being absent, Calvin returned to school and joined Year 10. He has a male classroom assistant who goes above and beyond his protocol. It is a huge relief to know he is being well looked after and supported at school. Calvin still has an eating disorder, but it is not as prevalent as it was in the early days. Football is his passion and he returned to playing football with a local club. He is a happy child and makes us all laugh with his witty personality. He talks positively about his future plans. As his mother, caring for him was truly a privilege.

On top of taking care of Calvin, I tried my utmost best to try to keep the house running, my business, Ross' baking, and looking after the needs of the other children and Roy. Despite being exhausted at times, I pushed myself somehow, getting the strength and energy to keep going.

After Calvin returned to school, I went back to my morning walks and indulged in my twice weekly circuit classes. At times, I even surprised myself, but I kept reminding myself that something 'good' had come from this. Calvin was getting better. I was living for today, not for tomorrow, next week, or next month. I was trying my best to live life in the present, capturing any fleeting moment of joy and happiness I could salvage.

Time to Pay

THERE ARE TIMES WHEN life throws you into situations that feel beyond your control, and this was one of those moments. The pressure was immense, and I often found myself overwhelmed by the weight of responsibility. Sleepless nights, endless worry, and the constant need to keep going, even when it felt like everything was falling apart, became my reality. More than just the potential loss of a house, it felt like losing a piece of our identity, a place that had been the heart of our family. The uncertainty was crushing, and the guilt weighed heavily on me. But through it all, there was a determination, a refusal to give up, even when the path ahead seemed impossible. I struggled to make sense of it all, trying to find hope in what felt like a hopeless situation. Yet, somehow, there was still a quiet strength that kept me moving forward. We held on to each other, to the belief that we would find a way through, and to the idea that sometimes, even in the darkest times, there is a glimmer of hope. It's a reflection on resilience, on the deep desire to protect what we love, and on the belief that no matter how hard things get, we can find the strength to keep going.

The time had finally arrived when we had to pay for that awful incident at our family home. I still remember my first meeting with our solicitor, who told both of us that we were going to be financially destitute for a very long time. Those words never left me, ravaging my mind and consuming my soul. When I left the care system, I had very little money to survive, but the difference was, I was able to control that situation and knew things would get better with hard work. With this situation, we had no control whatsoever. In the early days, my doctor prescribed me with anti-depressants as I was finding it incredibly difficult to process everything and deal with Calvin's illness. I decided against taking them in the end as I was too scared that if I did take them, I wouldn't function properly and really felt that I needed to have my wits about me at all times to navigate through the turmoil.

People told me, 'It's only a house, just bricks and mortar' and basically that it was 'no big deal' if we needed to sell our family home. It meant a lot more to me than that. It was our family home, where we had spent all our married life together with incredible and happy memories. We had built our lives around our home – school, work, church, walks, family, friends, activities, and we had the best neighbours that money could buy. You cannot put a price on any of that. Roy understood my desperation to keep the family home. Throughout my time in care, I had craved for a place where I could call home. Our family home had brought me stability, comfort, and security that I so desperately needed when I left care. The thought of ever losing it brought me so much heartache and pain.

Since the incident, we have sacrificed everything – family holidays, nights out, eating out, buying clothes, anything that required unnecessary spending was put on hold. We had no choice but to work every waking hour that God sent us, to save every penny we had. At times we both struggled to motivate ourselves to work, knowing that everything we earned needed to be handed over, as we desperately tried to keep our home. We were both mentally and physically exhausted, but we had no option but to keep going, propping each other up and holding onto one another for strength.

For a very long time, I carried so much guilt, blaming myself for getting our family into this mess and the suffering it caused. I was the one who allowed the insurance to lapse and permitted those seeking compensation onto our property during a fundraising event. This decision ultimately led to the incident and the resulting hardship we faced. Roy reassured me time and time again that it wasn't my fault. He was so desperate to fix the situation as he felt I had suffered enough in my younger life.

The whole situation felt like mental torture, consuming every waking hour I had. Some nights, I barely got four hours sleep, frantically waking up with it ravaging my mind. I had lost 'me' in all this, my radiant personality, sparkle, and zest for life.

But I couldn't lie down. I had too many people relying on me to carry them, but at times I just wanted to be carried too.

From the outset, we accepted liability. We were instructed to complete an affidavit, in which strangers scrutinised our financial worth. There was nothing we could do.

I questioned many times the scales of justice that are displayed outside of a courthouse, with their balanced sides that represents the principles of fairness and equality in the legal system. The symbolism of the scales highlights the idea that all evidence and arguments should be weighed objectively before a decision is made. As far as the law goes, we were liable to compensate the people claiming compensation. We felt we were being punished because we worked hard all our life and had bought and paid for our home. It felt unfair.

This heavy burden that I was carrying affected my physical health, especially my feet. Every inch they burned and ached with pain. I desperately needed my feet to be better, as walking is my passion and was my biggest escape from the nightmare.

A visit to a Kinesiologist told me my body was consumed with anger, grief and loss. I wasn't surprised. I suppressed my emotions, choosing not to go down the route of anger. I held no animosity, bitterness, or resentment towards the people claiming compensation. I just prayed for them and wished them every happiness in the world.

Throughout my heartache, my counsellor listened to my cries and woes but she was unable to fix my pain. She told me it was 'situational' and reminded me that I had amazing strength and resilience. There were days I didn't feel it but I kept pushing and clung onto hope we would get through it. Time and time again I reminded Roy and the children that everything was going to be okay. It was only money, but it was a substantial amount of money that we needed to find. I tried to stay positive, pushing through the uncertainty and stress, salvaging any happy times I could. My priority was to keep the family together and listen attentively to their struggles, while behind the scenes, I sometimes crumpled in despair. I hated seeing them suffer.

As a mother, I tried everything in my power to bring joy and happiness to the home, something we all desperately needed.

The incident had distorted our children's minds and, in my anguish, I tried to teach them to see the goodness in life and reminded them constantly that something 'good' would come out of this situation. A good friend of mine told me that "God gives His hardest battles to His strongest soldiers". I had been reliant on God's strength and grace to overcome this battle for so long. I cried so many times, begging God to give me the resources and strength to get through this pain. I prayed constantly and listened to the bible attentively with Father Mike Schmitz. I reiterated so many verses in the bible reminding myself that God was in control and HE was the only one that knew the outcome. These two were my favourites – *Matthew 11:28-30 Come on me, all you who are weary and burdened, and I will give you rest. Take my yoke upon you and learn from me, for I am gentle and humble in heart, and you will find resort for your souls. For my yoke is easy, and my burden is light. Proverbs 3: 5 Trust in the Lord with all your heart and lean not on your own understanding.* Throughout this big ordeal God remained faithful and gifted me with amazing strength and grace. I am so thankful for that.

After many years of trying to negotiate a settlement, Roy and I were both asked to attend the High Court in Belfast at the Great Hall with our legal representative and with the claimants' legal team.

While waiting for our legal representative to negotiate, I sat praying with my hands crouched on my knees. The tension and the pressure was unbearable, as this was a culmination of the case against us. Finally, an agreement was reached for the compensation claims. The settlements were guided by a book referred in Court as the Green Book which provides guidance on claim values in Northern Ireland. Finally a settlement was reached but it was for a very substantial amount of money. On the one hand knowing the outcome was a huge relief, however we still had a battle on our hands to find the money and to find it 'now'.

Leaving the court house our solicitor had told us that he and his wife had spent many a sleepless night worrying about us. We were both genuinely shocked when he told us. I had gone to that solicitor just before the incident to apply for compensation from the historical abuse scheme. Never in my wildest dreams did I think I would ever need him again so soon. No matter what time of the day or night it was, our emails and text messages were always replied to. We had the best solicitor and he always had our interests at heart. Really, we cannot thank him enough.

As well as paying for the litigation, we were responsible for everyone's legal fees. This money had to be paid within a tight timeframe. Our biggest worry was that we did not have all the money. We had our 'rainy day account' as Roy called it, our life savings and the money I received from the historical abuse compensation scheme. I grieved the loss of that money because I had to provide evidence to a mental health professional of the impact of the abuse I endured at the children's home. Mind you, I was so grateful I had the money and told myself it was money I was not meant to have.

With my expertise and skills, I embarked on my 'final' fundraiser. This time for our family, not for the charities and individuals who normally would have benefitted from my volunteer work. I felt really sad about that. As a family we felt absolutely awful that we had to resort to doing this. It took a lot of guts to do the fundraising but we had to swallow our pride no matter how proud a family we were. I was so determined to never give up and held onto hope that people would understand our situation and support us. We visited the bank and credit union to investigate our options for taking out numerous loans. It was such a worrying and stressful time. Just as we were about to apply for the loans, a friend came to our rescue and kindly offered us a loan with no interest and conditions. We were overwhelmed by their generosity and how desperate they wanted to help us. Sadly, it still wasn't enough. We were really looking a 'Miracle' to save our home.

I set up a GoFundMe page -

We are Roy & Isabel Kelly from Ardglass, County Down, Northern Ireland. It comes with great sadness that we as a *family find ourselves in the position of asking for your financial support, due to a tragic incident which occurred at our family home. Unfortunately, our insurance had lapsed and there is no insurance to cover a significant liability that has arisen in respect of this incident. On legal advice we cannot go into this in any more detail. **There is a real possibility that we could lose our home as a consequence of this incident.***

*The money raised will go directly to **deal with our liability arising from this matter.** We are contributing our life savings and need to re-mortgage our home to address this issue but we kindly ask for your help to raise the substantial sum required to address the liability.*

We are a proud family and feel absolutely awful that we have to resort to asking people for financial help, but sadly we have no other option. As you can imagine, it has been a very stressful and worrying time for all of us.

For the last 20 years and more our family have fundraised on a voluntary capacity for many charities, organisations and individuals. Never in a million years did we ever think as a family we would have to resort to fundraising for something like this.

As a family, we are deeply grateful for all the love, support and prayers offered and for all the help that we hope you can give. From the bottom of our hearts, we would like to convey our utmost thanks for your kindness and generosity. Please keep praying. We truly believe the power of prayer changes things.

All liabilities have to be settled by 31st August 2024.

Roy & Isabel Kelly x

Once the GoFundMe page went live on social media family, friends, and strangers kindly donated in their droves. So many families and friends had felt our pain and had journeyed alongside us for so long knowing what had happened. The outpouring of love and support was overwhelming and made us realise how well we were thought of, as a family.

So many people had reached out to us and wanted to help with the fundraising. I set up a WhatsApp group to let everyone know that I was organising an 'Afternoon Tea' at Roy's church, which generously donated the venue free of charge. I had previous experience in running this type of event over the years for many charities and it was always well attended. I suggested running a draw and literally within minutes people in the fundraising team were donating amazing prizes. The support was incredible.

The week leading up to our big fundraiser was manic. There was so much to organise and do. I was juggling so many balls, trying to run a home, work, do the baking for Ross' coffee business, finalise the publication of this book, and organise the fundraising. It really was a busy time but underneath I knew that we were finally reaching the top of our summit. Behind the scenes, I was battling to get the money together before the first and final deadline. My stress levels were at an all-time high with adrenaline pumping around my body at an extreme rate. I knew this was not good for my body and at times I tried different alternatives to regulate and calm my body.

Different people told me that they would crumple if it happened to them and would have no alternative but to sell their home. They told me that I was the only person they ever knew that would get through this and was fortunate to have the skills and know-how to do something like this. That was comforting and reassuring, but it still did not take away my worry. While people on a daily basis were living and trying to sort out their household bills, our challenges were so much greater and difficult to manage. We still had our household bills to pay and on top of that, find a huge amount of money within a tight timeframe. The extreme pressure took its toll on me and, at times, I found it so overwhelming and would break down in tears.

On the 29th of June 2024, we hosted our Afternoon Tea. We had a great team behind us preparing for the day and helping us to set up, serve tea, coffee, refreshments, wash dishes, and clean up. I honestly cannot thank you all enough as you were all truly remarkable and went the extra mile for us. I found it an extremely emotional day. So many people, far and wide, attended our Afternoon Tea and blessed us in abundance. The outpour of love and support was clear to see.

The stress and pressure we endured throughout this whole situation might well have broken up many a family. We, as a family, stayed together throughout this incident and are tighter knit than we have ever been. This proved to me as a mother and wife that holding onto faith and hope even in my darkest moments is a true testament of how far we as family have come and where we are today.

Through this ordeal, I learned a lot about the law, and I feel it is certainly not there to protect the people who work and try to make something of their lives. This incident has caused me to see the importance of insurance cover and I now frequently remind others to ensure their insurance is in order. I do not want to see others go through what we went through.

The 'Good' news is that we did indeed get our miracle! My meticulous planning of us both saving throughout our married life and the money raised from the fundraising contributed significantly to being able to keep our family home. We feel incredibly blessed and relieved our nightmare is over. We still have debt, but I know in my heart through time and hard work it can be paid back. I do not want to reflect on the "what ifs". I am living for right now and want to close this chapter in our lives.

Faith and Forgiveness

FAITH AND FORGIVENESS are themes that have shaped my life in ways I never anticipated. For many years, these concepts felt distant, words spoken in church, ideals that didn't seem to apply to the reality of the world I knew. How could faith exist in a place where suffering was so prevalent? How could forgiveness be an option when the pain felt so personal and deep? These were questions I carried with me for much of my life. It took years before I could understand faith beyond the confines of what I was taught, beyond the rigid traditions and rules that seemed to only make me feel more alone. There comes a point where you stop looking for answers outside and start turning inward, searching for something that brings peace amidst the chaos. In those quiet moments, I began to see faith not as something forced upon me, but as something I could rediscover in my own way, on my own terms.

Forgiveness, too, is a journey I resisted for so long. It seemed impossible to forgive those who had caused so much hurt, those who had taken away things that could never be returned. Yet, holding onto that pain was like carrying a weight that kept me anchored in the past, preventing me from moving forward. Slowly, I began to understand that forgiveness isn't about absolving others of their wrongs, it's about freeing yourself from the grip those wrongs have on you. In the pages that follow, I explore the complicated and often painful process of learning to trust again, of finding faith in the darkest moments, and of discovering how forgiveness, though difficult, can lead to healing. These are not simple paths, but they are ones that, in time, bring a sense of peace that I had long thought unattainable.

Barely an adult and reluctant to keep his daughter, my father was still capable to make the decision when he handed me over to the State to be a Roman Catholic. I doubt my mother had her say because, after all, she abandoned me.

Religion was a big thing in the late 1960's and early 1970's due to the Troubles in Northern Ireland where all-too-many Roman Catholics and Protestants were killing each other. Religion is merely an accident at birth. For a majority of people, their religion is something they are born into and brought up with. As a child, I had no choice over my religious affiliation. Baptism is the first sacrament that a person receives in the Roman Catholic Church. It is the entrance to all the other sacraments and is considered the foundation of the whole Christian life. The Roman Catholic Church believes that it is important for a child of believing parents to be introduced into Christian life as soon as possible. And even though I was a Roman Catholic, my father had not even bothered to get me baptised. It was picked up as not having been done by the baby home when I was twenty months, which is deemed relatively late in the Catholic Church. So, there I was taken to St Bernadette's Church, Belfast on 14th of December 1972 to be baptised and given a godmother who worked at the baby home.

Religion was shoved down my throat from when almost I could talk. After all, I was being looked after by the Sisters of Nazareth, a holy order of nuns run by the Roman Catholic Church. By the time I reached four years, I was attending Mass regularly in the chapel at the children's home and we were ordered as a group to say our prayers in front of the Sacred Heart of Jesus statue for thirty minutes every evening. There were holy statues and crosses everywhere around the children's home.

As a child, I often questioned my faith to myself. If God is good, why was he letting cruel and wicked nuns harm me? When I left the Children's Home in 1978 aged 7, I was fostered by a Roman Catholic family. I continued to go to Mass only because it was forced upon me, just the same as other Catholic families back then. Then, like all Roman Catholics, I made my First Holy Communion at aged 7 in 1978. First Communion is an important tradition for Roman Catholic families and individuals. It occurs only after receiving Baptism, and once the person has reached the age of reason, in my case it was 7 years. In keeping with tradition, the attire for the First Holy

Communion is usually a white dress for the girls with a veil and should serve as a little reminder that she is Christ's bride.[3] To mark this joyous occasion I wore a white long dress with a veil. While at primary school I auditioned to join the school choir with barely a note to my head and, to my surprise, was chosen. One of the prerequisites of joining the choir was to sing at Mass every Sunday morning. So, every Sunday morning I religiously walked to Mass and sang my heart out. I loved that time in my life as I felt I played an integral part of the choir and felt a sense of belonging. Sadly, I had to leave the choir when I left primary school.

In P7 aged 11, I made my Confirmation, another one of the seven sacraments that proceeds Baptism and Holy Communion. Confirmation is a sign that a person has reached maturity and is now able to take responsibility for their own faith. It takes place during a Mass that is given by the bishop. The bishop anoints the believer's forehead with holy oil called chrism. At confirmation you get to pick a middle name. I never had a middle name so I was rather pleased. I picked Therese.

Throughout my teenage life I continued to attend Mass every Sunday and on holy days either as a family or with the other children in the house. Sometimes I lied that I was at Mass. Instead, I was hanging around with other children somewhere else but I always made sure that I got the bulletin, news about the parish I was attending, as proof I was there.

Both the primary schools and high school I attended were run by nuns. Religion was an integral part of everyday life. We said our prayers together in class, attended weekly assembly in the school hall with prayers and readings, and prayers were delivered over the intercom before the school day finished.

Nuns were heavily present in my life throughout my childhood. A nun is a woman who vows to dedicate their life to a religious community, committing to the vows of poverty, chastity and obedience but live an active vocation of prayer and charitable work. Unfortunately, most of the nuns I met were

---

[3] (Source www.catholicgallery.org)

wicked people and as a child, I could not fathom to understand how they belonged to a religious order. In my experience, Nazareth Lodge was a place of fear, hostility and confusion, where I was degraded with impunity. Sister Angus was the cruellest nun I have ever known. She showed me no compassion, love, kindness, or patience. She often told me I was the Devil's child in her raging voice and screwed-up face.

When I joined my new primary school, I was met by an angry and disgruntled nun who was the principal. She was such an ignorant and dismissive nun who had no time for children and should never have been in that role. She hit me hard across my bare hands with a metre ruler which really hurt, as I was disruptive in class. Then I came across more nuns at high school who took their anger and frustration out on me yet again. I remember one nun in particular who hit me hard across the head with her knuckles, repeatedly, for not understanding the subject. In my defence, I used to raise my hands in the air due to fear and to try to stop her from hitting me across my head. My head used to throb for ages because it hurt so much. Another nun expressed her frustration because we were rushing our prayers at Mass, so she made us repeat the prayer slowly for ages.

By the time I left foster care, I was a non-practicing Catholic. I resented the Catholic Church due to the outrageous suffering it caused me in the hands of specific individuals within the Church. I was adamant that if I had any children they were not going to be raised as Catholics. It caused me so much anger, distress, and pain that it seeped through my whole body. And even though I still believed in God, I struggled to comprehend how he could allow my suffering. If only I dealt with it back then.

Around 1992, my foster parents received a telephone out of the blue from police wanting to interview me regarding historical abuse. I thought it was to do with the nuns at Nazareth Lodge. As a child I rarely spoke about my time in Nazareth Lodge or about the abuse as I blamed myself, nor did I ever think anyone would believe me. It turned out the police were investigating a Catholic priest called Brendan Smyth. I had no recollection of him. Father Brendan Smyth was a convicted sex offender from Belfast, Northern Ireland, who became a notorious child molester using his position in the Catholic Church to obtain access to his victims. He was the first paedophile priest to scandalise the Catholic Church in Ireland. Spanning forty years, Smyth sexually abused and indecently assaulted at least one-hundred and forty-three children across multiple parishes in Belfast, Dublin and United States.[4]

It was a horrific thing that happened to these children and it was very brave of them to come forward. That gave me hope that one day Nazareth Lodge might be investigated.

Even though I was not a practising Catholic I still believed in God and occasionally prayed to Him. In 1997 aged 26 I was preparing to get married. Roy, my husband to be, had asked me if I would consider going away to get married because he did not want any fuss and it would be easier because we were marrying into a mixed marriage – Roman Catholic and Protestant. It felt a little like the dark ages. I loved the idea. So, in a moment of madness, we booked to get married in Barbados. It sounded so idyllic and I never gave any thought as to what the Catholic Church would think. Roy was very keen to get the marriage blessed by his Minister at his Church on our return, inviting family and friends. Things started to stir up inside me realising that I should get our marriage blessed by the Catholic Church.

I was really upbeat when I contacted the local parish priest, thinking what I was proposing would be a walk in the park. However, everything that I had conjured up in my head was totally different to the outcome that I would receive from the parish priest. He was horrified to hear that I was not getting married by the Catholic Church. He was not having any of it and told me abruptly that our marriage was not recognised by the Catholic Church and every time that I took Holy Communion at Mass, I was a sinner. For me that was taking it to the extreme.

---

[4] (Source – www.Wikipedia.org/wiki/Brendan_Smyth

To soften the wound, he informed me that he would bless our home, but nothing else. His response threw me into disarray. I fully accepted that our marriage was not recognised by the Catholic Church but to call me a sinner played havoc with my mind. Was that a man-made rule as it certainly was not in the bible. As far I was concerned, we were all sinners and who was he to preach at me? His affirmation confirmed to me that I was not welcome in the Catholic Church. I was bitterly disappointed and disgusted by the way I was treated. His reaction made me resent the Catholic Church even more. If only I had the guts to tell him about my past events with the Church!

At last, there was justice. People were coming forward to speak about the historical institutional abuse they encountered. In 2014, The Northern Ireland Executive's Inquiry and investigation into Historical Institutional Abuse examined if there were systematic failings by institutions of the state in their duties towards those children in their care between the years of 1922 to 1995.

The Inquiry commenced its public evidence sessions with an Opening Hearing on the 13th and 14th of January 2014 at Banbridge Courthouse, Banbridge, Co Down, Northern Ireland. The independent inquiry into historical institutional abuse formally closed in June 2017 after two-hundred and thirty-three days of hearings.

The inquiry investigated twenty-two institutions in Northern Ireland, as well as the circumstances surrounding the sending of child migrants from Northern Ireland to Australia, and the activities of the late Father Brendan Smyth, and the issues of finance and governance. Nazareth Lodge was one of the institutions who were found to have abused destitute children (Volume 3, Chapter 9, Module 4 Sisters of Nazareth, Belfast, Nazareth Lodge 97 pages). I hadn't taken part in this inquiry but attended the public statement on the publication of the Historical Institutional Abuse Inquiry report at a hotel in Belfast on January 20th, 2017. It was a proud moment for me as it reaffirmed that it was not a figment of my imagination and the physical and emotional abuse that I endured was true. The truth was now public knowledge.

Thankfully, through God's sovereign intervention, I found faith in him again aged 43. Something miraculously happened to me when I was on a thirteen-hour flight from Dubai to Sydney. God literally reached into my life and asked me where I was and that I should go back to Mass. His voice was so powerful and it rippled throughout my whole body. In one split second, beyond a shadow of doubt, I knew God loved me, and that he had a plan and purpose for my life.

I returned to the Catholic Church four weeks later on my return from holidays and I have never once looked back. When I returned to Mass in 2014, I was absolutely lost because parts of Mass recited by the congregation had changed. These changes were made on the First Sunday of Advent 2011. The new translation was a much more faithful rendering in English of the third edition of the Missale Romanum (the definitive Latin text of the Mass and its associated prayers), promulgated by Pope Saint John Paul 11 in two-thousand and one.

The new translation of the text of the Mass sounded a little foreign to my ears as I had grown accustomed to the older, looser translation. I was determined to learn the new translations and stay faithful this time. Through time, God was working through me. I was like a real pro and learnt really quickly. I love going to Mass and being close to God. It turned out that I actually did need God in my life and I was only punishing myself all these years holding some much anger and resentment against those people who made my life miserable.

Then, in 2018, Tierna and Craig had left the Protestant church they had been attending to join a new Church that was more modern of its time. I was witnessing big changes in their spiritual lives and wanted what they had. I was curious to find out what their new Church was like so I decided to take myself to their service every Sunday night while attending Mass in the mornings. The atmosphere was electric and I could feel the Holy Spirit's presence. At times, I would cry during the service as it stirred up emotions I had suppressed for years, which were now beginning to resurface. For the first time in years, I started to openly talk about my past to people I met at this new church, and friends. I was hungry to grow my faith and attended the

Alpha course, prayer groups, bible groups, prophetic and worship nights, as well as regularly attending Mass.

I realised that I could not change the things that happened to me in my past but I did know I had some freedom about how I was going to respond to them. Although I needed some kind of help, I was exhausted carrying this heavy burden. In April 2019, God placed this before me and directed me to Theotherapy counselling, a modality of Christian counselling that uses biblical principles to bring about renewal and transformation of the mind. The counsellor told me in order to be free and move on with my life, I had to forgive the people who I needed to be free from. Forgiveness is the act of pardoning an offender.

In the Bible, the Greek word translated "forgiveness" literally means "to let go," as when a person does not demand payment for a debt. However, in light of our new beginning, God commands that in return, we forgive others and extend grace as we have been shown grace. The pain and hurt others cause us is real and great. Jesus used this comparison when he taught his followers to pray: "Forgive us our sins, for we ourselves also forgive everyone who is in debt to us." (Luke 11:4) Likewise, in his parable of the unmerciful slave, Jesus equated forgiveness with cancelling a debt.—Matthew 18:23-35. We forgive others when we let go of resentment and give up any claim to be compensated for the hurt or loss we have suffered. The Bible teaches that unselfish love is the basis for true forgiveness, since love "does not keep account of the injury."—1 Corinthians 13:4, 5.

The counsellor told me that when we forgive others, we are not saying what they did was okay, but we are releasing them to God and letting go of its hold on us. In my fifty years of being on this planet I never once thought of forgiving the people who caused me so much pain. It was the furthest thing from my mind. I was too fixated on the past wounds and with the people who inflicted these. Some of these people probably did not know exactly how their actions had affected me. But keeping all my wounds raw, hardly warranted that those people will ever accept responsibly for their actions. I understood what forgiveness was but the realisation of actually doing it was another matter.

Getting my head around it was very difficult but I knew for me to be free I had to accept and be ready that I was willing to forgive. At different times in my life, I had dwelled on hurtful events and situations far too long, often placing my life 'on hold'. Gripping on to bitterness and grudges was never my intention but I had two choices, either to keep going down the route I was going or forgive and lead a much better life. With the support of the counsellor, I was able to identify what needed healing and who I thought I needed to forgive. Of all the people I conjured in my head to forgive it certainly was not my mother and father. It had not occurred to me that they needed forgiveness. Digging up old wounds, I soon realised that I was holding onto so much anger, resentment and bitterness. I felt my mother had failed me terribly by not being present ever in my life and depriving me of the love that I so badly needed and craved. My guilt with my father lay in the fact that he handed me over to the State, never fought to keep me and never came looking for me.

I have finally accepted that awful things did happen to me, and I realised what people did was not justifiable, excusable, or all right. By choosing to forgive and release feelings of anger, resentment, and bitterness, I no longer hold on to what happened or blame the people who caused me suffering and pain. Through the process of forgiveness, I have recognised the true value and rewards. Forgiveness has helped free me from the control of people who darkened my life. It has helped me develop greater understanding, empathy, and compassion for others. Notably, it has helped me to feel better about myself, physically, mentally, and spiritually, and to have healthier relationships. When negative thoughts enter my head now, I try to bring it back to the present focusing on what I am doing or keeping myself distracted. Forgiveness is a process, and even when hurt runs through my head, I revisit those and continue the process of forgiving over and over.

As part of my forgiveness process, I shifted my priority to self-care. On a daily basis I continue to nurture myself emotionally, physically, spiritually, and mentally. I try to surround myself with positivity and supportive relationships, concentrating my positive energy on the people close to me that I love and who love me back. I have created a nurturing environment for my personal growth and well-being to celebrate my freedom. I engage in activities such as walking, circuits, writing, reading and kayaking. These bring me so much joy, laughter, and satisfaction.

Since returning back to my faith I have continued to look forward to life ever since, finding more goodness and beauty of God than I ever dreamed possible. On a daily basis my faith continues to grow as I draw closer to God through prayer and the study of His word, the Bible. I respond to what God has done for me by putting my faith into action and living as God instructs me to live in the Bible. When life is going well, I know it is easy to feel like God is on my side and that he is working on things in my life for good. I am so thankful to God for everything and tell Him that every day of my life.

Going to Mass is an integral part of my life. I try to go to Eucharistic Adoration every week. The Eucharistic Host is displayed in a monstrance on the altar so that everyone can see and pray in the presence of Christ. The first time I went to Adoration many years ago, I stared closely to the monstrance where it started to sway from right to left continuously, moving around the very spot where it was located. I know I could only see it but it felt as if the Holy Spirit was delighted with my presence and was putting a cloak around me to protect me. To this day, every time I go to Adoration the same thing happens to me.[5]

After all these years we are getting married AGAIN! I had raised it many years ago with my current parish priest of my experience with the former parish priest objecting to 'Blessing our Marriage' because we were not married in the Catholic

---

[5] Looking back all these years I have no regrets bringing the children up as Protestants. We tried our best to integrate the children as much as possible and I feel this has played an integral part in their lives, learning to accept people, irrespective of their religion. This has really made our kids who they are today. It's something that we all need to do in Northern Ireland.

Church. He felt at the time I was too hurt by the Catholic Church and left it until now. He suggested we have a "Convalidation ceremony".

A convalidation is when someone has been married civilly, but due to an impediment the marriage was invalid as a sacrament. The impediment must first be removed, and the couple then makes a new exchange of vows to enter into a sacramental marriage. The usual impediment would be what's called lack of canonical form which is when a Catholic marries outside the Church without permission. In such a situation, a new exchange of vows is performed in the Catholic form in order to make it valid. The process to have a civil marriage validated in the Church is essentially the same as any other couple getting married in the Church: Provide sacramental records, evidence/testimony of freedom to marry in the church, copy of civil marriage, normal pre-marital paperwork, and exchange of vows before Catholic clergy and two witnesses.[6]

It means a lot for me to get our marriage recognised by the Catholic Church and receive the Sacrament of Marriage. My faith is integral to who I am as a person and my beliefs. I am so grateful to my parish priest who all along waited for the right time in my life to suggest this to me. Really his timing was perfect!

A week after my 50th birthday, sitting out on the patio enjoying the sunshine, Roy asked me "would I do anything differently with my life?" I had to think about that question because at that moment I felt very content with my life. Mind you, that took years of counselling, discussions with Roy, and self-care. I cannot change my past nor do I want it define me. Digging a little deeper I wished that I had the support from professionals in my teenage years to deal with my trauma and feelings of rejection and abandonment rather than letting it escalate for a further three decades. But the biggest thing for me is that I wished I had forgiven the people who had caused me so much suffering and pain much earlier than I did.

---

[6] (Source www.catholic.com/qa/convalidation-process)

As much as I would like to be healed from trauma and be done with it, trauma does not work like that. The truth is that I will never really get over it as my mind and body do not forget. The purpose of my healing was for me to accept the events that happened and to learn how to manage and cope with my feelings and thoughts. Triggers and reminders of my trauma still provoke emotional reactions, even today, but that's okay. I now have the tools and skills to continue my recovery and healing. Despite the challenges I faced, healing from my trauma has been possible for me. It has been a journey of self-discovery, resilience, and transformation. Along the way, I have learnt to develop self-care and self-compassion and prioritise my own well-being. I refuse to be defined by my past or confined by the restrictions of trauma. For me, I have embraced the fullness of life, with all its joys and sorrows and found meaning and purpose.

You are probably wondering - what was the turning point in my life? I never had that 'epiphany moment'. The trouble began when I was born. My life was not straightforward, but it rarely is for people. I was unlucky not to get parents who were eager and full of energy and a wider family circle who could take up the slack when they were not. Everything that was taken away from me, I slowly got it back, BIT by BIT. For me the one thing that I always had was HOPE. I never knew it as a child but I do know now that I am survivor and have found my voice. Is-Abel I am.

Reflections

In my scant leaving care records that I eventually got four decades later read:

31/01/78 Social Worker visited the three children. General discussion with the three children about their understanding about being in Nazareth and future plans. Isobel said that she had never lived anywhere else (other than Nazareth). Isobel said she had never met her mummy and asked if she could go and see her. Social Worker discussed with Isobel how her mother was unwell and therefore not able to look after them. Isobel then asked if she could go and see her mother when she grew up. Social Worker agreed this would be possible. Discussion with all three children about Court. Children were aware that some other children in Nazareth had been down to Court and then went to live elsewhere. Discussion re the role of the Judge in deciding their future. Isobel was her usual, chatting, questioning self.

14/03/78 Court Hearing—Parental Rights Order obtained. My mum, grandfather and uncle, attended court. My father sent in a letter explaining that he had no objections to the arrangements at Court. The children appeared fairly settled but at times appeared edgy and nervous. Isobel appeared cheerful and talkative and appeared to like talking to her uncle. She remained in high spirits. The children had to wait from 10.30am-2.30pm. They played with books and read all day. They behaved very well considering the length of time they had to wait.

Joanne's Interview

I MET ISABEL in High School. When I moved house nearer to where Isabel lived, I got to know her better. I found out then that she was fostered. I often wondered what had gone on in Isabel's life that had brought her to foster care. I didn't dwell on it very long as our school lives and personal lives got in the way. I knew nothing about the care system—only that my uncle and aunt fostered children who lived in Dublin and it was never discussed. Upon getting to know Isabel at school, I noticed how immaculately dressed she was with tight, curly hair. She bounced around the place and was full of energy. She was somebody who was a leader and had to be in the thick of things. Isabel only really talked about her life in care years later after we left school. It was at her and Roy's blessing that her real mum was there. Gradually, over the years, she opened up more freely and talked about her experience in the care system. Our relationship did not undergo any alterations because of Isabel's upbringing in the care system. Isabel left a lasting impression on me. I have great admiration for her, especially when she took herself to Guernsey on her own. She just got up and done it and never give it a second thought. She is a strong person and has a successful life whatever she has gone through. She is hardworking and whatever comes her way she gets up and brushes herself down—she is a tough nut.

Roy...

I HAD HEARD ISABEL was fostered before I met her. Rumours had circulated amongst the locals that the family going to be my neighbour across the road, fostered children. I was intrigued as I had never met a family who fostered children before. I met Isabel for the first time in a group of children at her family home, but I took no specific notice of her. When Isabel and I started a relationship, I was interested in how it affected her being fostered and not being with her real family. My main concern at the time was that Isabel may not reach her full potential long term because of the effect of being in care.

Since I met Isabel, I have a much better understanding of the care system, how things are dealt with by the social workers and some frailties in the system. Having to deal with Isabel's insecurities, jealousy and trust issues put a strain on the relationship. I thought the arguments we had were petty and had done my head in. I did not navigate through them very well because of a lack of empathy. It was only when we got married that I realised the stupid arguments we had were down to what Isabel had been through and how deep Isabel's problems were as she was trying to deal with them.

Through our relationship, I have tried to guide Isabel with other relationships and when to give up and to never let it rule her life. Isabel always looked for more intense relationships that she would never get back. Our own relationship suffered at times because it was intense and I could not cope with it, but we got through that. Despite the challenges that Isabel endured, I persisted with the relationship because I knew she had a lot more to give and could not bear to not be there, to not see it happening. The one thing that has stood out for me about Isabel is her zest for finding out what life was really about. She had the passion to make life better for herself and those around her. It is all or nothing with Isabel. She has a way of doing things and never faffs about to achieve it. She doesn't let people stand in her way.

The one good example of this was when our youngest son Calvin was gravely ill with an eating disorder. Isabel went to extreme lengths to educate herself about an eating disorder, seeking private help for Calvin and took him privately to get diagnosed with his autism. Despite the experts who were more interested in getting him to eat, Isabel questioned everything and took her own path and got him on the road to recovery. She could identify the 'time wasters' and filtered them out, never afraid to let people down or felt bad. When the time came to return Calvin back to school after being off for a year, Isabel researched the support he might be entitled to, applied for it and dealt with the mountain of paperwork and assessment meetings. She never took her foot off the pedal and fought his case the whole way, successfully securing a full-time classroom assistant for him.

Past Colleague and Friend Interview

I FIRST MET ISABEL in a professional capacity when she was my boss, then as the years progressed, we became and continue to be friends. After building a relationship with Isabel for 18 months at work, we were having a conversation one day and she told me about being brought up in the care system. I was shocked, saddened, and intrigued. Our conversation led me to try to understand what she had been through, as I couldn't imagine it. To hear her personal story made my brain to go into overdrive. I asked a lot of questions as I was trying to process the information and understand her story. I was in my early twenties then and was naïve and very sheltered about an individual growing up in the care system, but I had great sympathy. Finding out about Isabel's story helped me to understand some of her characteristics, such as determination, resilience, highly driven and openness. These characteristics taught me a lot, starting out as a fresh graduate.

In a professional capacity, Isabel gave me a lot of her time and helped me to gain a strong work ethic that I still adhere too. She led by example and was highly dedicated to her family whilst still being a career woman. Isabel left a forever impression on me. Her dedication to her family, her work ethic and total readiness to help anyone that needs help regardless of what's on her plate, her level of energy, her outlook on life, her positivity, her extreme generosity and thoughtfulness. Through no fault of her own, Isabel has every right to be cross with certain aspects of her life but chose to turn that around and be positive. I only had to mention something and she offered a solution. After twenty-four years of knowing Isabel, I still have great admiration for her and what she had been through.

Gillian's Interview

I WAS NEVER CONSCIOUSLY aware of Isabel's existence before initial contact was made. I was never told of Isabel's existence but there was a photograph displayed of three children at my granny's house. I was told it was three kids up the street. But when Isabel made contact with me in March twenty-eleven the photograph made sense.

I was so excited and intrigued when Isabel reached out to me. I found her very welcoming, very friendly and professional. I was happy to have gained a cousin. My initial motivation to remain in contact was how we got along and delighted to hear Isabel's perspective, as I only had the experience of my own family experience.

Isabel's experience in the care system made a positive impact on her as it made Isabel who she is in terms of how much she helps people and her determination. She has a broader perspective of her life with her experiences.

Everything about my darling cousin has left a lasting impression on me. She is highly focussed and driven despite everything she has been through and is extremely resilient.

Alison's Interview

I WAS AWARE of Isabel's existence. I knew Brian had children in care. There were a lot of secrets and dysfunction going on. The first time I met Isabel I thought she was absolutely bonkers and very open. There was a real sense of wanting answers and she asked a lot of questions. I definitely think she had a real need to belong, especially with attachments that impacted her life in care. Upon meeting her for the first time, I really thought she was outgoing, friendly, very open and willing to talk about her journey. There was definitely a feeling of connection with the both of us and I liked her openness. I wanted to stay in contact with Isabel as I really liked her, she had similar morals to myself and she was on my level which is very difficult to find in a person. I had been searching for family myself and having that connection with a new family member brought me closer to her as we have a lot of similarities having faced adversity and trauma in our lives. We are both very funny. Isabel most definitely left a lasting impression on me. Her resilience to overcome adversity though not unscathed, but to a level of being successful. She is able to pick herself up and is a strong person.

Kevin's Interview

ISABEL AND I were both fostered, by the same foster parents. Isabel was sixteen years older than me. I very much perceive Isabel as a member of our family. Isabel's presence contributed significantly to my life. I always looked up to her as my big sister. She has had a big impact on my life. I was always doing things with her from a young age. She was always there to guide me and teach me, especially about working hard and being nice to people. Isabel is very kind, funny, loving, caring, hardworking, genuine, supportive, and a trustworthy person. She is a great listener and good at giving advice. Isabel has left a lasting impression on me. She always wants to thrive, do her best and has a good head on her shoulders. I felt I had to do the same so, I copied her!

Epilogue

TODAY I LIVE NEAR Ballyhornan. The shop and petrol station lie empty and run down, with a 'sold' sign displayed outside. The RAF base closed abruptly and without warning at the end of the 1990s. The former RAF accommodation at Ballyhornan has changed into residential accommodation, bringing new life to the village. As an adult I am a frequent visitor to Ballyhornan as our son Ross runs a mobile coffee trailer business – 'Kellies Coffee' located at the carpark. I still walk the beach and occasionally visit the billets where I once spent my summers away from the confines of the children's home. Every time it takes my breath away, bringing me back to my childhood and the fleeting moments of happy times I had.

My dream is to walk part of the Camino de Santiago, otherwise known as the Way of St James. It is a network of ancient pilgrimage routes from across Europe to the tomb of St James in the Cathedral of Santiago de Compostela in Galicia, located in the northwest of Spain.

My desire to help others has never left me. Who knows where my journey will take me? But, for now, I am still breathing and really am so grateful as I still have so much to live for.

Useful References

Bowlby, J. (1969). *Attachment and Loss: Volume 1*. Basic Books.

Dozier, M., & Rutter, M. (2021). Attachment-Based Interventions for Children in Foster Care. Development and Psychopathology, 33(2), 241-256.

Goldman, J., Salus, M. K., Wolcott, D., & Kennedy, K. (2022). A Coordinated Response to Child Abuse and Neglect: The Foundation for Practice. U.S. Department of Health and Human Services.

Greeson, J. K., Usher, L., Grinstein-Weiss, M., & Gross, J. (2023). Supporting the Transition to Adulthood for Youth Aging Out of Foster Care: Evidence from Longitudinal Studies. Children and Youth Services Review, 141, 105-115.

National Youth in Transition Database (NYTD). (2021). Outcomes for Youth in Foster Care. Washington, D.C.: U.S. Department of Health and Human Services.

Perry, B., & Szalavitz, M. (2021). The Boy Who Was Raised as a Dog: And Other Stories from a Child Psychiatrist's Notebook. Basic Books.

Pecora, P. J., Kessler, R. C., O'Brien, K., White, C. R., Williams, J., Hiripi, E., ... & Herrick, M. A. (2009). Educational and employment outcomes of adults formerly placed in foster care: Results from the Northwest Foster Care Alumni Study. *Child Abuse & Neglect*, 33(1), 59-72.

Steele, H., & Vaughn, B. (2020). The Impact of Childhood Trauma on Adult Attachment Styles. Journal of Child Psychology and Psychiatry, 61(3), 201-210.

Tuan, Y.-F. (1977). *Space and Place: The Perspective of Experience*. University of Minnesota Press.

Printed in Great Britain
by Amazon

51011662R00091